101 SHORT LESSONS for an ANXIETY FREE LIFE

LESSONS

To my son, who showed me that fear is only as powerful as I allow it to be.

INTRODUCTION

This is a book for individuals concerned with anxiety. Both those looking to prevent anxiety, and those currently living within the grips of an anxiety disorder. It is to teach us that in order to become more than our anxiety, we must become greater than our irrational thoughts, greater than our feelings, and greater than the identity we believe we need to hold.

It is easy to act on the established thought patterns we hold in our minds, and therein lies the problem: it is much easier to act on these established patterns than it is to create new ones. The challenge arises when we are forced to reflect on them, question them, and defy them. Through this book, you will be challenged to do exactly this. To question your behaviors, your thoughts, your anxieties. To be brutally honest to yourself why you picked up this book and ask the difficult questions about what has truly stopped you on your path to inner peace.

I will not give you the answers to your questions, but rather I will guide you to ask better questions of yourself.

Through this series of 101 daily lessons, I will reveal how what you think is the cause of your anxiety is only a symptom of something deeper. Something that needs to be revealed, acknowledged, and addressed before it is healed.

The best way to go about these daily lessons is to read one lesson each day upon waking up in the morning and applying the teaching to that particular day.

Uncovering the roots of your anxiety will be a long, potentially difficult task. And the best way to approach it is through gradual, bite-size steps. The daily lessons within this book are designed to break down this behemoth task and guide you through the challenges you meet in a series of accessible, thought-provoking lessons.

Think about it like climbing a ladder. Each day you will be given one piece of mental guidance. As you reflect on it, see how it applies to your life, and apply the teaching in a way that feels unfamiliar and new, you put yourself in creation mode. You allow yourself to establish new thought patterns, rather than falling back down the easier, well-worn path of repeating the damaging mental patterns from the past.

As you progress through the lessons, you will see I regularly refer to the unconscious mind, the conscious mind, and the intuitive mind. These concepts can be translated in this way:

Unconscious mind (the inner child):

The unconscious mind is your most loyal servant. It does everything it is programmed to do—for better or worse. It will strive to protect you from anything that may come into conflict with its programming unless the "conscious mind" convinces it that a change is necessary and safe to adopt.

The unconscious mind, in essence, will hold onto things until the conscious mind steps up and tells it what to do with it.

- This is your "mental iCloud," an immense storage system located within your brain and body. It is your filtering system, and it always takes the path of least resistance.
- Every piece of data received through any of our five senses is stored within our unconscious mind for recall and review.
- It is the 'inner child' within you that often screams the loudest.
- It is the single, most powerful goal-achieving agent known to man.
- It is a poor decision maker but it is great at running automatic patterns so that the conscious mind can handle other activities that need conscious handling.
- It is stuck and unchanging. If its childhood programming established the idea that your identity was connected to being an underachiever, lazy, ugly, or otherwise, the unconscious mind would do everything in its power to match these programs later in life.
- It has the cognitive rationale of a 10-year-old who has been built up through first instances, memories, decisions made, and actions, and it groups things by what's familiar.

Key understanding: Rumination is nothing more than an overactive unconscious mind asking questions that the conscious mind hasn't answered yet.

Conscious mind (the decision maker):

The role of the conscious mind is to be the decision maker. It is responsible for giving orders to the unconscious mind. However, it is not the most proactive element of the self, and will often allow the unconscious mind to make its own instinctive reactions. If no direction is forthcoming from the conscious mind, the unconscious will act out of habit or according to someone else's directions.

- The conscious mind is the rational, analytical part of the mind. It's the thinking, judging part of the mind.
- It is the least informed and the last to know what's taking place.
- It is analytical and thinks in facts and figures.
- It has a weak and finite memory system in contrast to the powerful and unlimited capacity of the unconscious mind's permanent memory.
- Unlike the unconscious mind, the conscious mind—the decision maker within us—uses up 'brain juice'. That is until the old mental and emotional recordings become drowned out by updated perceptions, thoughts, and belief systems. Automation occurs just as it did in the past during periods lived with stress and anxiety.

Key understanding: Healing is changing old perceptions stored within the unconscious mind so that they sing in harmony with a newfound conscious intent. It is not a matter of a person winning a battle with inner voices through the mustering of will.

Intuitive mind (intuition):

Like an ocean where the unconscious and conscious selves are the drops that make up the ocean, the highest self is the ocean itself. It is the part of you that knows rather than thinks it knows. It is the part that has a hunch when something is right or wrong. Your intuitive mind is the part of you that feels connected to everything and pulls you to flow with the ever-changing aspects of life. It is your intuition.

- The self, the source of individual life, purpose, and expression.
- The god within.
- It gives guidance, wisdom, and inspiration, but does not give orders.
- It is the seat of our intuitive abilities.
- It is composed of your thoughts, emotions, and actions, as well as the people around you, and together allow you the access you have to your intuitive mind, the mind of manifestation.
- It is an infinite field of potential.
- It is responsible for the transition from vision to physical reality.

Key understanding: The intuitive mind uses the memory stored within the unconscious mind as a pattern or blueprint to create an equivalent physical experience.

The journey to anxiety-free living takes practice.

If at any point you would like to repeat a lesson for one or more days, you may do so. There are no set rules on how to approach the contents of this book, only personal guidance from me on how I believe the best path forward could look. In some lessons, you will find sections that dig deeper into the content. You can read these at your leisure, or find out more on my various channels.

Let us begin with our first lesson now. Approach this first lesson with an open mind, an open heart, and patience. Together, we will simplify the path forward to inner peace and work toward becoming more than our anxiety.

Blessings.

Dennis

LESSON 1—

THE UNCONSCIOUS MIND REVEALED

The unconscious mind is the seat of your memories and core beliefs and it is responsible for your immediate reactions to an event. These reactions can come in the form of a feeling, an immediate act or behavior, a verbal expression, or even the idea that pops into your mind. These reactions are learned and cemented during childhood.

During childhood, the unconscious mind receives all its information from the 5 senses as fact and acts accordingly. It is obsessed with closure and will do everything in its power to find or supply the answer to any question it faces, regardless of its positive or negative outcome.

However, if an answer is brought forth consciously and it does not align with the core beliefs held within the unconscious mind, it may be rejected until more evidence, consistency, and emotional backing behind the evidence is brought forward.

All core beliefs held by the unconscious mind come with a certain degree of motivation to keep them there. An important reason, or reasons, for keeping them alive.

The intuitive mind is your connection to the source: your heart sense or intuition, the part of you that gives guidance and inspiration but not orders, and the part of you that knows rather than thinks it knows. Intuition can also be referred to as the 'god head' or the 'god within'.

Your intuition knows that you are not your mind. You simply have a mind, just as it knows you are not your body but rather you have a body.

In my personal world, intuition is treated like an inner being.

In between these two minds, we have the conscious mind, or the 'decision maker.' The decision maker is responsible for the amount of willpower you put forth towards an act, where you place your conscious attention, and the amount of rational thinking you bring to an experience. It is your internal processor and makes decisions on behalf of your conscious mind.

Lesson 1: Dig Deeper

What is held in memory and core belief systems shine through the mind through repeated mental chatter, physiological symptoms such as sensations, pain, aches and diseases, dreams, Freudian slips, and the imagination.

It's important to note that the messages from the unconscious mind are not intended to lead our thinking and actions. Rather, they are sent to the decision maker, the conscious mind, so that it can decide what to do with them. For example, when your unconscious brings forth a new physical symptom, such as a restrictive feeling in the throat, most people don't see it as information from the past looking for resolve in the present. Instead, most people will get frustrated over the symptom (hence contributing to the build-up of tension in the body), and look for the fastest cure to take it away (often through a technique they've never used before or a pill).

If only the decision maker could step in after the initial message and project a more curious response to the symptom, the person would understand that the fear of speaking up has a very good chance of being the culprit. If this were to happen, change would begin to occur. Verbal expression will begin to overtake suppression, and soon enough the symptom will no longer have a reason to show up.

However, this doesn't mean the entire anxious and fear-centered program run by the unconscious mind is now replaced. It just means that a certain degree of negative emotional baggage has been let go of, and the unconscious mind has begun to ask more questions through the mind and body while the decision maker must be prepared with an answer.

It's important to understand that not all answers sent from the conscious to the unconscious mind come through some change in behavior. Some answers can be given soapily through the practice of in-action. For example, when the unconscious mind projects its fear-centered program through spontaneous itching in the body during a conversation. The itchiness is a call to leave the conversation, so when the conscious mind decides to ignore the symptom and continue to engage in the conversation with positive emotions flowing through and out of them, all of a sudden a signal of safety gets sent back to the unconscious mind. Now the next time these two people meet, the itchiness will have lessened dramatically because the unconscious mind is no longer sending the message through the body to leave the environment.

If we continue doing what we've always done, the unconscious mind will continue to believe that whatever programming came from the past is still the way to approach life today. This is where the conscious mind comes into play. As we reveal the truth behind the messages from the unconscious mind, we can begin unraveling the old programming and replace them.

Over time, as the conscious mind takes the leading reins on how best to live life from the unconscious mind, intuition will begin to play a greater role in the person's life as well since there is now space left over for all three: the conscious mind, unconscious mind, and intuitive mind. This congruence between the 3 minds creates an inner harmony that leads to a 'flow state' in the individual. The unconscious responses to events are no longer led by irrational fear and a need to protect from something or pressure the old memories and core beliefs. Rather, the immediate responses align with safety. The key here is to understand and rebuild the delicate relationship between the conscious and unconscious minds. Being stern with your unconscious mind in moments where it is needed is fine, but any disappointment, hatred, or anger response to an unwanted idea or feeling will only strengthen the core beliefs that are centered around fear and the illusion of separation.

We now understand deeply that what we concentrate on, we get. Therefore, through re-identifying with the help of the decision maker, we can begin concentrating on creating the kind of inner world we want to have and therefore have our external world match that new frequency we are giving off into the world.

LESSON 2—

YOU ARE NOT YOUR THOUGHTS NOR YOUR BELIEFS

We now know that we have in and around 60,000 thoughts per day, and as you can imagine most of them are repeated ideas spurred on by the unconscious mind. However, we mistakenly begin to believe that these ideas are our own and that we must hold some level of value for them.

That is, until the decision maker puts forth a new idea that counters the habitual one or chooses to no longer act in line with or become emotionally invested in the original idea.

Repeated thoughts in and of themselves are nothing but mental patterns that have become unconsciously strengthened over time.

There is space between a familiar thought and a frantic reaction. Space to understand that the thought is the unconscious mind's cry for resolve rather than a demand to be followed. Anxiety sufferers often cannot see beyond the intrusive thoughts and immediate feelings because they are completely out of rapport with their unconscious selves.

As we divert our energies away from the immediate fear-centered emotion and toward becoming the witness of the element of anxiety, we begin taking its power away. Interestingly, the decision maker may even ask such questions in those very moments of an intrusive idea arising such as:

- Is this thought mine, or a product of someone else's belief system?
- Why does my unconscious mind feel the need to share this idea (or feeling) right now?
- How appropriate is this idea for this current situation?

These sorts of conscious questions show us that we can think beyond how we used to think about ourselves and life as a whole. The unconscious mind needs and craves direction from the conscious mind, the decision maker. If there is no direction given it will get it from other people: fear looks for more fear.

However, on the opposite spectrum, love looks for more love. By allowing the conscious mind and intuitive mind to guide the unconscious mind, we can bring love into the picture towards that which we've feared for so long.

Lesson 2: Dig Deeper

In a house full of adults, it's the baby that screams the loudest. As the mental and physical body begins moving from franticness to calm, the baby's unconscious mind will feel threatened by such a drastic change in being. The screams through mind and body will become very strong at this point, and as the individual continues to be the witness of the screams, the screams become less bothersome. And as the screams become less bothersome, the need for the screams will become less needed.

This all comes from a place of love.

The power struggle between the unconscious mind and the decision maker begins shifting towards cooperation at this point. During this transition, the unconscious mind may attempt to caution you with warnings such as:

"If you let your guard down something bad will happen, and it will be your fault!"

However, the power struggle is shifting toward cooperation. Although the unconscious mind applies labels these labels, it's important to remember that the unconscious mind remains open and willing to change its old ways. It's just hesitant.

In the beginning, the hesitation shows up in the form of intrusive ideas and feelings. These then clarify in the mind and ultimately cleanse the body through a new default emotional state. Once we no longer identify with the old meanings we've placed on things, along with these outdated thoughts, we open ourselves up to the energy of creation.

The voice from the unconscious mind will no longer drown out the guidance voice of the intuitive mind, and not knowing the true answer to something no longer comes with pain and struggle. Rather, we let things be, we let things go, and we let ourselves see the imperfect perfection in everything about us and this world.

LESSON 3—

THE BODY ALWAYS KNOWS

Dissociation is the feeling of being outside of what is presently taking place. A single traumatic event, or repeated events, along with a chronically stressful lifestyle can lead a person not only to suffer from anxiety but also to become dissociated altogether. The body does this so that it can dampen the impact of the traumatic event and protect you from whatever challenging and similar events may arise in the future.

This leads to an inability to feel emotions, mood swings, forgetfulness, irrational behaviors, and the inability to focus our attention on one thing.

Hyper-fixation of this physiological phenomenon leads the self to justify all of the fear-centered perceptions held within the unconscious mind.

It is at this point that we must be attentive to the messages the body is sending rather than be flustered by the symptoms it is experiencing. Herein lies the key to deep inner healing: an attitude of empathy for what the body is projecting. Without the proper attitude toward what has brought us to a place of chronic anxiety, there can be only symptomatic relief during healing interventions.

Hence the pendulum-like experiences that anxiety sufferers go through between symptom progress and setbacks. It is not the skill set or guidance from others that has failed, but rather the attitude of the individual. The path forward hasn't been placed in our hearts and projected forwards in all we do. There is no foundation for healing.

Equipped with this new understanding and attitude towards the body we can begin to reverse our mindsets and even our hypersensitivity. This happens as we mentally and physically rest and allow the mind and body to project whatever it wants to. The tight hold over our bodies is no longer present as the physiological tension begins releasing.

We then realize that all our previous attempts to forcefully alter something we don't want to feel have only fed into the anxiety.

As we give up trying to control the health of our bodies through willpower we feel a certain metaphorical nakedness arise. This experience may lead people back to what was once their comfort zone of fear. However, we must understand that the nakedness is our true selves, the self that goes through life with effortless effort. Never pulling only to have the desire move farther away, and never pushing only to have it be front and center in all we do.

This new empathetic attitude towards the body's projections allows our symptoms to move toward intuitively dealing with anxiety, rather than intellectually looking for a systematic step-by-step approach.

Remember, there is no separation between mind and body. They are one and there is a continuous feedback loop between them. Alter your overall mental attitude towards the body's symptoms and the body will in turn project safety where there was once relentless fear.

LESSON 4—

DO LESS FOR ANXIETY AND YOU WILL HEAL

If anxiety is on the mind, anxiety is in the body. If we make personal changes for the purpose of taming anxiety then we are only feeding it more. The "doing" becomes useless. However, once we begin to make changes for the purpose of re-connection we begin to truly heal anxiety. This distinction is vital for our healing.

Every meditation session therefore becomes an opportunity to connect with the unconscious mind in a deeper way.

Every old fear-centered thought that is replaced with a non-threatening perception is now for the purpose of updating the beliefs of our own inner child.

Every action that is slowed down rather than sped up due to anxious habit is now to move our attention from close-minded threat to open-minded safety.

As you can see, although all of these inner changes help to release anxiety, none of them are for the purpose of releasing ourselves from anxiety. If our total focus is on healing anxiety we will always be focused on symptoms, bodily or otherwise.

We must go deeper than this. We must explore the deeper motivations stored within the unconscious mind that keep the elements of anxiety alive.

This explorative approach isn't something we sit down and analytically try to organize in our heads. It is something that we feel out gradually in order to develop a new relationship with mind, body, and spirit altogether. It is imperative that you ask yourself the questions—the brutally honest questions—about what it is you are trying to achieve through your personal change work. If you are happy with your results, meaning the state of your mental, emotional, physical, and spiritual bodies, then you are likely approaching your change work well. However, if you find that you are not where you would like to be, then it is time to focus less on what you do and more on the reasons why you are doing them.

Making personal changes is about re-connecting with our unconscious mind, and through reconnecting with our unconscious mind we can begin to heal.

LESSON 5—

PAST RECORDINGS LOOK TO CONFORM TO PRESENT REALITY

Often we think about the root causes of our anxiety in terms of what happened to us. Many of us believe that it was our childhood traumas that created the blueprint for how we see the world today. However, this is only partially true. In truth, the root cause of our anxieties is the way in which we recorded what happened to us and not the event itself. Our recordings create the meanings that we unconsciously experience in the present day.

If we continue to see the roots of our anxiety as things that happened to us, we will forever be pointing the finger at others and looking for an answer outside.

Two separate individuals can have the same childhood experiences and yet have two completely different ways of perceiving the past. As a child, the experience was simply something that happened rather than something to protect against. When the experience shows up again as an adult, our unconscious mind urges us to protect against it. It's important to understand that these root experiences are just recordings and that we have the ability to change them as we please.

Years of talk therapy to deeply understand our past traumas can now be replaced with the understanding that what we do in the present can alter the way we recorded what happened to us in the past.

For example, if there is a person in your life right now who is a trigger for anger and fear, your present strategy may very well be to avoid this person at all costs. In doing so you are only justifying the fear-centered recordings in your unconscious mind that are connected to the original event that linked this person to the anxiety you are looking to escape from today. Instead of running, understand that the fear and anger triggered are simply relating information to your past, and your unconscious mind has chosen to work with the ingrained emotional reactions instead of rerecording events.

This doesn't mean forcing yourself through the interaction with this person on a regular basis. That would only provoke more physiological tension. Rather, notice the tension in your body during the build-up to meeting this person and mindfully let the tension go. During the conversation, slow down and instead of suppressing your creative ideas, share them in a confident manner with the belief that what you have to share matters deeply to the world.

These changes will begin the process of re-recording the actions of the original event that began the hypersensitivity. As time goes on, blame and regret transform into sympathy and understanding.

LESSON 6—

HEAL THE HEART AND NOTHING ELSE

In this book, you will hear the term 'elements of anxiety'. This refers to different ways in which anxiety manifests in a person's life; the internal reactions to the perception of threat and the patterns of stress that have accumulated within the system.

Since a person's external reality is also a mirror of their internal reality, the blocks in relation to fear can be seen vividly in different areas of life. Sometimes there is a financial unreservedness to create more sources of income, or maybe a person continuously finds themselves in abusive relationships. These have less to do with luck and everything to do with the energetic output we are giving off through our feelings from one moment to the next.

Anxiety can manifest in many internal and external ways. This leads us to believe that we must micro-manage each 'problem' that shows up either as an internal element of anxiety or some type of external situation.

In truth, it is the heart that needs reflecting upon in order to see what is being held there, who it believes we are, and what it believes we deserve.

The heart gives off its own electromagnetic frequency. This frequency also manifests as what I call an 'information grid', more commonly known as an aura, that emanates outwards from the spinal cord to up to 8 feet from the human body. The moment we have an emotional shift, whether positive or negative, the information grid surrounding us shifts to create a change in how we perceive, feel, and sort out the information gathered through our five senses. Therefore, it is vital to understand that the only change that needs to happen is a change in the heart.

We must become who we are working to become prior to releasing what it is we are looking to release.

Anxiety makes us believe that we cannot allow our conscious or intuitive minds to lead our lives, and this is simply fear finding more fear. In truth, an idea is just an idea, a bodily sensation is just a bodily sensation, and your immediate reactions to an event are simply warning signs coupled with question marks built to protect from the unconscious mind.

Healing the heart begins with softening up towards ourselves.

If your heart has experienced something once, it can experience it again. As we explore and begin to make changes to what the heart has held onto for so long, we can begin to see through our old patterns and begin to ease back into playfulness, gentleness, and allowance. No longer is there a need to struggle or be punished prior to receiving some type of reward. The reward is in letting go, and the eventual champion will become once again.

LESSON 7—

YOUR THOUGHTS DO NOT REFLECT YOUR REALITY

Often when we think that we are thinking, we are simply remembering an idea we repeatedly acted on and believed was true before. True thinking is, in fact, an act from the conscious mind—the decision maker—and not the ideas that arise from the over-protective unconscious mind. Worse, an idea from the unconscious mind often comes with many other similar ideas, like branches from a tree.

This never-ending loop of ideas keeps an already busy mind busier in the hopes of the continued activation of the fight or flight response, a response that can even become habitual. They are not to be seen as real thoughts—or habits—but distractions from potential real thoughts.

The unconscious mind is extremely hesitant to allow the conscious mind to decide the meaning of things, and thus fuel behavior.

Hesitant, yes. Unwilling to ever give up the reins to the decision maker? Not necessarily. Anxiety recovery is a convincing game and you will never meet a more stubborn opponent than your own unconscious mind. It will fight tooth and nail to hold onto what it believes is true. It is also very opportunistic, as the unconscious mind will sense a lack of sleep or a missed meal and use it to make you believe, once again, in old fear-centered ideas that used to keep you so intimately connected to anxiety.

Imagine for a moment an overbearing mother who hovers around you at every turn, looking to keep you safe from potential predators. Now multiply this feeling of suffocation by a hundred, and you have your unconscious mind. But, remember, it is not your reality.

Once we learn to separate an unconscious idea from a conscious thought, we take a major step forward in our anxiety healing.

This cannot be done only once and celebrated. This is a lifestyle pattern. However, you may get to a point, as I have, where you begin to laugh at any negative, catastrophic, or pessimistic ideas that are spurred on by the unconscious mind. Once this becomes a genuine habit, you are leading rather than being led by.

This transition of power occurs once the intuitive mind is given the green light to interact. Once this happens, harmony begins to occur between instincts, intellect, and intuition, and these systems start to work the way they were originally meant to: congruent with one another.

You are not the ideas that cross your mind. You are the thoughts you consciously inject into any given situation.

LESSON 8—

THE MANY FORMS OF FATIGUE

Not all fatigue is created equal. There is such thing as good fatigue and bad fatigue. Good fatigue arrives through dedicated inner work and contribution to the world. Bad fatigue arrives through a hardened, forceful, and selfish approach towards life. One leads to a feeling of elation and victoriousness while the other is towards helplessness and self-victimization.

Only a truly honest person who has gotten themselves to 'the point of no return'—complete dissatisfaction with the results they are getting—can begin noticing the differences between these two types of fatigue.

In turn, you must see what direction your current fatigue is taking you. Good fatigue will lead to purpose, elation, and increased energy while bad fatigue signals that it's time to 'gear down' and place boundaries on certain aspects of your life. This signal indicates that you have crossed the threshold of what your mental, emotional, and physical body can handle.

Bad fatigue is perpetuated by forcefulness and a bullying approach to getting what we want.

This adds to the accumulated tension in the body, hence the mental concerns that begin showing up in regard to the health of the physical body. Physical symptoms begin to travel from one part to another and grow in strength, acting as a message to the conscious mind that if this attitude towards life is continued it will only fuel more mental, emotional, and physiological anxiety.

Good fatigue is only temporary. It lays the foundation for creativity and purpose. As the tight grip over life is let go, the body will start to tire. And as you regain your energy, you regain a zest for all things in the present and future once again.

LESSON 9 –

THE PAST NEEDED TO HAPPEN THE WAY IT DID

Whether your past was filled with positive or negative experiences, understand that it needed to happen the way that it did. Our upbringing provides us with the information that we can reflect upon and use accordingly in the present, and this information is needed in our adult lives. A truly loving upbringing and family dynamic help us to perceive things in a light-hearted way while a challenging upbringing shows us how easy it can be to fall into the trap of fear.

Both are good. One is not better than the other, it is all information.

The problem arises when the individual justifies their present anxiety by pointing the blame onto others from their past.

As mentioned earlier, fear looks for more fear, and blame will look for more blame. If only this same individual could see the motivations influencing their unconscious mind to keep an anxious state alive and become open to perceiving life through the eyes of those very authority figures from their past, they could begin the healing journey. However, often the comforts that come with anxiety—or the secondary gains, as psychology calls it—become all too familiar in the face of inner change work.

If you've had a rocky past growing up, understand that there is a part of you that still clings to those experiences. Our job now is to understand that we are made up of many parts and we get to decide which ones to strengthen and which ones to weaken.

Any part of you that clings to the past to justify present anxiety can and must lose its power over you. This is done by first accepting what took place and then by entering into your 'afterlife'. Right here, and right now.

The afterlife I refer to is the life after the one that was programmed into you during childhood. I am talking about fear (past life) vs unconditional love and surrender (present and future life).

We even have the potential to change our wordings from calling past experiences 'traumas' to calling them 'experiences'. You had experiences, not traumas since trauma tends to come with a clinging feeling while experiences are more fleeting. They come and they go. The question is, starting today, how will you begin viewing your past?

LESSON 10—

'DOER-SHIP' IS HOLDING YOU BACK

There's 'do-ing' and there's 'doer-ship'. You may do something nice for someone and expect nothing in return, or you could strengthen your doer-ship qualities by doing something nice for someone and expect an immediate return. Perhaps you only allow yourself to feel a high degree of self-worth and self-love after having achieved a certain amount of income, gained a certain amount of followers online, or heard a compliment from someone else. This would fall into the category of doer-ship, and doer-ship is holding you back.

Doer-ship is the manifestation of someone who 'gets the job done, never takes no for an answer'. Someone who doesn't give up on the goal they have set for themselves until it is achieved. Interestingly enough, however, anxiety healing is one of those things where the attitude of doer-ship perpetuates the perceptions of present and future threats and dangers rather than resolves the anxiety riddle.

The term doer-ship is one you must familiarize yourself with and hold yourself accountable to. It is character traits and mental habits connected to:

- Forcefulness
- Impatience

- Conditional self love
- Perfectionism
- Self-punishment patterns
- Superiority thinking
- Greed.

The important thing to note here is that it's not a question of doing or not doing. It's about how you go about what you do. As we keep a very close eye on the unconscious mind and its tendencies, we may notice doer-ship creeping in at work, at home, or right after we wake up in the morning.

As the rush of anxiety-fueled adrenaline hits, we find ourselves exercising at a frantic pace in order to release the pent-up negative feelings that are stored deep within us. We must slow down as by slowing down, we can begin seeing things more deeply.

As we slow down, we notice that exercise can be enjoyable and pleasant instead and that it doesn't have to always be connected to a specific goal or outcome.

This is when the habits of doer-ship begin to slowly take a back seat to open-heartedness. These are the very moments when we begin to break old patterns that were knowingly or unknowingly installed into us by the world.

The important thing is to see doer-ship in what you do, what you say, how you perceive, and how you interact with the person you see in the mirror each morning. Most importantly, it is how you imagine the future.

LESSON 11—

CREATING PROBLEMS WHERE THERE ARE NONE

How often do anxiety sufferers fall into the trap of thinking they have to change everything about themselves, followed by changing everything about other people? When in an anxious state, our perceptual filters will sort for what is or can go wrong in the world, therefore neglecting what could go right until the conscious mind gets involved in the mental decision making. In short, while suffering from anxiety we tend to find more and create problems that never existed.

Take, for instance, an anxiety sufferer taking a shower. The analytical mind will question whether the water is hot or cold enough, whether they are standing in the shower correctly, how long they should be showering, and whether they used too much or too little soap on their body.

This is a good opportunity to remind this person that it doesn't matter how they shower, as long as they are having a pleasant experience.

This shift in emotions from mainly negative to mainly positive allows us to re-program the heart toward love and safety. We must become more mindful and recognize when we are creating a problem where there is none. Moreover, we must not place this mental behavior under any kind of label toward ourselves. Rather, we must promote positive patterns that lead us to think in a positive way, and that is all. Patterns can change as long as the new direction is repeated with a degree of certainty in them.

Since worry has been a constant companion for quite some time now, we tend to revert to it most prevalently when we are engaged in something different. That is, until different experiences are moved through with a level of safety and trust that we can be fully present within them. We are the creators of our problems, and we are the only ones that can take them away.

LESSON 12—

EVERY EXPERIENCE DEMANDS A NEW MEANING

Our immediate feelings and sensations allow us to quickly gauge whether we hold safety perceptions or threatening ones toward any experience. However, these are not the elements that decide the meaning of a new experience. This is done through the conscious mind, and over time gets relayed to the intuitive mind. If we judge a new experience by what our unconscious mind makes us feel, we may decide to run from, fight back, or even freeze in the everyday situations we encounter. That is why we must no longer believe our initial feelings in any given experience we go through during the day.

Imagine a person gets into their car and gets that dreaded feeling that they have to confront their boss at work again. They have two choices here: either they go along with the dreaded feeling or they use their body, followed by her mind, to alter the images of catastrophe that are running through their mind in those very moments.

So they slow down. They begin breathing through their diaphragm. They begin to notice that these ideas aren't their own, but are being sent from their unconscious mind. They then unconsciously begin to imagine their rapport with their boss in a positive way. Yes, her bodily sensations may still be present as she drives herself to work. However, the meaning behind these sensations is no longer true as the conscious mind, the decision maker within them, has shown up and placed a new meaning over a future event.

As often as you can, change the meaning of an experience by altering aspects of the body, and the breath, and soon the mind will follow suit. Do not engage in a tug-of-war of thoughts with your unconscious mind.

Sometimes a positive mental replacement isn't readily there, but there is a more neutral stance towards what was once a catastrophic future experience. Understand that this stance of neutrality is also a win for the conscious mind, another aligning of the three selves towards balance and safety.

As meanings get altered, the frequency we give off changes. The compounded stress from the last dozens of years of your life begins to be released from the heart, and the heart in turn emits a new frequency.

Change meanings as often as possible and watch your life experience shift as well.

LESSON 13 —

WHY YOUR ANXIETY SYMPTOMS ARE ALWAYS FRONT AND CENTER

It is more important to understand what perpetuates anxiety symptoms than it is to get to the exact root cause. The presence of bodily symptoms of anxiety comes down to a few things:

- Repressed and/or suppressed negative emotions stuck in specific areas of the body
- A lack of true verbal, creative, or emotional release that gets held in the body
- Physiological signals from the unconscious mind that are relayed to the conscious mind as a potential threat, whether present or future, real or imagined (hyper-sensitivity)
- A sense of mental and/or emotional overwhelm that trickles into the physical body.

The reasoning behind this is that many anxiety sufferers who look to 'figure it all out' are only doing more harm than good for themselves, since mentally willing themselves to find the cause of the anxiety symptoms will only add to the physical tiredness and overwhelm long term. Couple this with making the physical symptoms your main focus of attention for the majority of your day, and your energy is suddenly knowingly and unknowingly being focused mostly on the very source of your issues: your anxiety.

The unconscious mind is always relaying messages through bodily symptoms to the conscious mind.

Therefore, it is up to us to see these symptoms as messages and not physical threats. When the unconscious mind begs the question, 'What do we do with this information, do we continue to hold onto it,' the decision maker must reply in a way that puts the unconscious mind on the path toward letting go of what's been held onto for quite some time now.

A frantic reaction to a bodily symptom only justifies and reinforces the fear-centered belief that came through as a bodily symptom. By allowing this symptom to manifest, we are basically replying, 'Yes, we must continue to hang onto this and believe in the core belief you are relaying to me through this symptom.'

The moment the anxiety sufferer makes their relationship with their unconscious mind their priority is the moment true healing begins.

Often the answers are right in front of us, but we are blind to them because of our mental fatigue. Anxiety makes us feel like we always have to go looking for something, and that answers cannot be held within. We must become open to the messages from the body and allow it to focus our attention where it needs to be focused.

LESSON 14—

LEARNING TO SAY NO

Our desire to please others often comes from the fear of rejection and the craving for acceptance (which we will touch on in later lessons). Therefore, in our anxiety-filled minds, saying no to someone is the same as letting someone down. Worse, it is a risk of alienating or separating from them. As a result, we refuse to say no, and in turn, this perpetuates the anxiety symptoms that arise in these situations. These patterns often have their roots in childhood abandonment and perfectionism.

However, remember that being alone does not necessarily mean loneliness. Your connection to your unconscious mind, the earth, and your source energy can easily take the place of any relationship that you have now outdated—that is to say, the relationships you recognize as being time to move on from. As you develop a new frequency, your new 'vibe' may require, or even attract, a new tribe.

Saying no makes us feel very vulnerable at first. However, over time, our levels of self-worth grow.

As our level of self-worth grows we realize that we are more capable than we first thought. Capable of of healing our bodies naturally, capable of becoming our own boss, capable of naturally attracting the kinds of people that align with our new belief systems. You become more capable in every way. The question is, starting today, what do you need to begin saying no to? The answer, followed by the repeated act of saying no to what you need to, will set you free.

LESSON 15—

YOUR PRESENT ACTIONS WILL HEAL YOUR PAST

Every heartbeat has the potential to emanate information and desires into the world. And every heartbeat brings back feelings and experiences of the world around us. Think of it like a boomerang: what you throw, you receive. Therefore, each new thought, emotion, verbal expression, behavior, or conscious or unconscious mental image has the strength to take us down a completely different life path than the one we've been on.

The challenge comes down to the way our unconscious mind likes to run things. The unconscious mind prioritizes familiarity as familiarity is safe.

However, with the knowledge that defense mechanisms will inevitably arise during any sort of change work, we can non-forcefully continue to act in opposition to the screams of fear emanating from the unconscious mind. By opposing these fears, we open ourselves up to the possibility of rerecording the unconscious memories, and in turn, aligning the unconscious, conscious, and intuitive minds toward one congruent path. Toward inner peace.

Inner peace doesn't mean that we are nonreactive, numb to the world, or that we must live as monks do. It means that we are no longer tied to the past programming and past meanings of all that life has to offer. Every new act has the potential to turn into a new program. This is the power of neuroplasticity, and we are capable of it at any age.

Your only limit is the amount of value you continue to place on fear and worry.

It is not the fear of death that fuels a hypochondriac. It is the sum total of all present actions that are motivated to find our true identity that has, once again, led us to a life we've been too fearful to live up to now. For example, the fear of revealing our true selves to the world has, once again, allowed fear to reject family, friends, and life.

Without sacrifice, there can be no change. We must be willing to give up what or who we've been clinging onto for far too long if we are to have a life that is more open-minded and open-hearted. This is the way to true inner freedom.

LESSON 16—

MASTERING EFFORTLESS EFFORT IN ALL YOU DO

Bodily tension is one of the biggest culprits of many illnesses in today's world. If you ever take the time to watch little children playing with one another, you'll notice how everything has a flow to it. There is no rigidity, stress, or tension in the children while they play, nor while they look to problem solve. If they can't find an answer to something they use the words 'I don't know.' These words do not need to be feared, and yet many anxiety sufferers have a hard time saying them.

We must get back to effortless effort if we are to break free of the mental rigidity and physical tension we have grown so accustomed to as adults.

This is why children are the greatest teachers we could have. They show us how we've strayed so far from our true essence. We must be more open and willing to learn from them than to continue to feel the need to teach them the ways of an adult. Effortless effort can therefore be put into practice in all areas of life, such as:

- Finances—Fighting for the next big pay raise less and more expecting it to be there in the future when the time is right.
- Relationships—No longer needing to be a part of every new piece of news that your friends come upon, but rather allowing the world to unfold as it may.
- Driving—No longer gripping the steering wheel so tightly, but letting go of the tension and embracing the flow.
- Meditation—No longer needing immediate calmness in body and clarity in mind after a meditation session is finished, but allowing whatever result meditation has produced and to allow it to be there, even if the mental chatter or physiological symptoms get stronger afterward.

Effortless effort goes against the orders of the unconscious mind to stand guard at the doorway of your mind and body at all times, just in case a threat appears. It does not come naturally. And to be honest, how could it? In school, we were never taught how our mind and emotional states dictate our external reality, nor how to manifest our goals without the need for pain and suffering through the process.

Now, however, we've grown to understand that the way we've been doing things in the past has gotten us a result that we are no longer pleased with, and we are opening up to a new way of doing things.

LESSON 17—

YOUR SENSITIVITY IS A BLESSING

We are now coming to understand that the root source of suffering from anxiety is closely linked to taking orders from the unconscious mind. As these orders are followed, the person may find themselves becoming increasingly fearful and sensitive towards people, environments, and new experiences.

However, the unconscious mind is not a simply cursed remnant of the reptile brain. We must also understand the blessings that the unconscious mind offers to highly sensitive people (HSP):

1) **They can intuitively sense into other people more than the average person.**
   In this way, they can sense what a person within their immediate electromagnetic field is thinking and emotionally feeling. In this sense, the HSP can provide support through their words, thoughts, or even just their intention, and make an immediate positive impact on the other person.

2) **They are much more mindful of the messages coming from the physical body.**
   As the unconscious mind provides valuable

information to the decision maker, the sensitive person can gently respond. For instance, in the past, you may have felt like you've been bullying your mind and body into feeling differently. Now, however, your sensitivity is playing an important and positive role in understanding and re-directing any past fears, suppressed negative feelings, or messages of overwhelm coming from the unconscious thoughts of the body.

3) **Your sensitivity fuels your vivid imagination.** We can use this to our advantage now that we have placed a few positive elements to our sensitivity. Rather than unconsciously imagining the worst possible outcome and continuing to live by our past trauma events, we can begin imagining something different. As we close our eyes, and relax the mind and body, we are immediately taken from a beta brainwave state (fully engaged in the day's essential activities) to an alpha state (where creativity and manifestation begin). From this place, we can begin imagining the past differently. We can ask questions like, "If I could go back and change this past experience what would I like to see, hear, feel instead?" As we run these vivid pictures or movies through our mental imagery, we release ourselves from the way we negatively encoded past experiences into our physical bodies.* As you build the skill of conscious imagination the way you feel overall towards the world will change.

This lesson needs to speak to you deeply as we no longer have to be the victim of our sensitivity but rather see the good within it. As we focus on the good aspects we can lessen anxiety at all levels which will lead to positive momentum over any future irrational fears we may come across.

*Look up ‘emotional reframing by the anxiety guy’ on YouTube for a guided session by me.

LESSON 18 —

YOU ARE ONLY MOMENTS AWAY FROM TRUE ANXIETY RECOVERY

Often when we are faced with a host of mental, emotional, or physical elements of anxiety we give up hope of fully being healed altogether. You must dismiss this thought. In truth, no matter where you are in your life right now, you are always one moment of progress, one behavioral accomplishment, one epiphany, or one piece of supportive information away from gathering recovery momentum.

To do this, our definition of recovery must change from needing psychological and physiological perfection to embracing repeated progress.

You are recovering when:

- Your old irrational fears no longer hold control over your conscious attention.
- You no longer look to protect your body from all possible external invaders such as peoples' presence and words, outside influences, germs, environments, or any kind of new experience that may lead to some type of physical tension.

- You become mindful of outside influences for healing. Retaining a paranoia over what every external piece of data may do to your body will only keep anxiety alive. The difference is in the approach.
- You wake up and automatically begin seeing the positive potentials in the day rather than all the things you need to become aware of in order to protect yourself.

Your path to recovery comes from turning the page on your fear. Move away from the unconditional fear (anxiety) and toward unconditional love (highest self). Stay open to this perspective and good things will start coming your way.

LESSON 19—

DENIAL IS THE BIGGEST OBSTACLE TO INNER PEACE

Denial is to declare something untrue, so we must ask ourselves how denial may play a part in keeping us stuck in an anxious loop. During my years living with a multitude of anxiety disorders, for example, I always denied that my physical symptoms could be the result of something other than a physical illness. The logic behind this wasn't right, but since worry was such a big contributor to what I thought was keeping me safe, I kept denying any answer that didn't take into consideration a medically verifiable physical issue. Denial held me back from recovery.

Most people believe that their anxiety began from an experience during adulthood when, in truth, often the anxious cycle begins before the decision maker was fully developed. This happens between conception and about the age of 5, meaning that many of us develop anxiety from our childhood experiences.

Of course, the memories of these root causes of anxiety are now out of reach to many of us without some type of mild to deep hypnotic work. However, the denial of this possibility altogether may keep an anxious person from looking into the places that represent the deeper root cause.

Another form of denial is denying that many of us today have become mirror images of someone from our past. Our authority figures and parents were the role models of how to function and think through life, and we tend to enact the behaviors that they enacted regardless of whether they were positive or negative to our well-being. Until we reflect inward and follow up by admitting to ourselves this truth of our denial, we will not be able to broaden our perspectives in regard to our overall healing.

The question is, what are you denying in your life right now? What do you need to admit to yourself that will potentially change the course of your life for the better?

LESSON 20—

AFFIRM YOUR TRUTH CORRECTLY

Affirmations have been around for a millennium, if not longer. However not all affirmations are made equally and we must first understand what aspects of an affirmation contribute to a positive manifestation and, crucially, the lack thereof. In this regard, we're talking about the elimination of anxiety altogether.

Affirmations are direct suggestions that often get repeated in the hopes of embedding the message into the unconscious mind. They do not work if we are evaluating whether they are, in fact, working or not. However, affirmations do work when we are suggesting new ideas in the present or present progressive tense. For example, using words in your affirmation such as 'in progress', 'achieving', 'creating', and 'happening'.

These words are 'power words' during affirmation work.

In progress — "My anxiety healing is now in progress because I deserve to feel true inner peace."

Achieving — "I am now achieving my ideal mental state because I value mental clarity."

Creating — "I am now creating only positive emotions because I deserve to feel great."

Happening — "My anxiety healing is happening now because life supports me in every way."

But there is also an important element that you'll notice in all the examples I've just given. The use of the word 'because.'

When we add the word 'because', the statement becomes a cause and effect statement. The cause starts at the beginning and the effect is at the end. Cause and effect statements have a much greater chance of re-teaching the unconscious mind since there is simple, clear reasoning behind the statement.

Remember, the whole journey to anxiety recovery is a conviction game and the re-building of the relationships between the unconscious, the conscious, and intuitive selves.

Therefore, we must understand what type of language the lower unconscious self understands and take note accordingly as we go forward.

Affirm with repetition for as long as you feel an emotional connection to the words and use these principles to allow progress to come to you rather than you chasing after it.

LESSON 21—

TO ADMIT YOUR WRONGS IS TO BE RIGHT

Many anxiety sufferers worldwide have very fragile levels of self-worth. Where this fragility derives from is always up for discussion, however, I'm sure you who are reading this book can guess where I believe the roots of this lie: I believe our authenticity left us many years ago through the corrective words and behaviorisms passed down from our well-intentioned authority figures. These led us to develop an identity that is more aligned with how others want us to be rather than who we ourselves truly believe we are.

The result is that to admit our wrongs is to make our projected identity vulnerable to dissolving itself. Therefore, the unconscious mind will keep us from making this 'mistake' as often as it can.

To admit our wrongs when the opportunity arises is to re-ignite our true authenticity. Over time, we discover balance in how to perceive ourselves. When this balance is found, the rigidity that comes with preserving an artificial identity begins to dissolve for good. Yes, it may feel strange. You may initially feel a certain degree of weakness.

However, in the long term, this openness to admitting your past and present wrongs will help to heal anxiety for good.

Remember, it's ok to be wrong, it's ok to admit your past 'mistakes', and it's ok to feel weak, negative, or victimized from time to time. It's ok to be human once again.

LESSON 22–

PERFECTION IS FEAR

Perfection is associated with the fear of getting it wrong, of letting people down, of not living up to expectations either from yourself or others. In my second book, *F*** Coping Start Healing,* I touch on this 'program' that runs in the minds and bodies of many anxiety sufferers today. I dig into the idea that, after some time, an anxious person will become convinced that it's the perfectionism program that has become the main contributor to the success the person has achieved in certain areas of their lives, which only strengthens the belief that perfectionism is a good thing.

However, this program leads us to become very 'touchy'. We feel like we mustn't feel the bodily sensation that we feel, we mustn't experience the intrusive thought that arose, or we mustn't be criticized by others or become engaged in any form of personal conflict whatsoever.

At this point, it is the decision maker—the conscious mind—that must come to terms with the idea that it was never the perfectionism program that contributed to the rewards felt in their career, relationships, or elsewhere.

These successes were due to the mental images of how they wanted that part of their lives to look like, their dedication to the end goal, and the amount of importance they placed on this success. The decision maker must let go of perfectionism.

Letting go of perfectionism looks like this: When you make a so-called 'mistake' of any sort, you respond to the initial feeling of doing something wrong with love, a smile, and gentleness. By doing so, you send the signal to the unconscious mind that mistakes are ok and they are not the end of the world. This is the beginning of the end of the rigidity and tension in mind and body that had been fueled by perfectionism for years.

Allow yourself to be less perfect, more real. To be less analytical after a social encounter, a speech, or otherwise, and be more focused on the present moment. Perfectionism, like other unconsciously-led programs, can subside, disappear, and be replaced over time.

LESSON 23—

THE DEATH OF YOUR REPUTATION AND YOUR PRIDE IS THE BIRTH OF YOUR INNER PEACE

You've grown so accustomed to who you've become today that you can no longer see how artificial this identity really is. It doesn't have flow, it fears any brainwave state other than high beta, and it looks to preserve itself at all costs. This need to preserve your pride and the reputation you've built up is not only an indicator of anxiety but also what keeps it alive for too long.

Your reputation, pride, and identity within the family dynamic, at work, or any other area of your life must be reflected upon and bared to its full nakedness to see how it is contributing to your anxiety.

To eventually allow your intuition to play a major role in your life, you must be first willing to let go of who you think you need to be daily. You must first change how you interact with yourself before others can change how they interact with you.

As pride dissolves, harmony begins to form between the unconscious, conscious, and intuitive minds. The minds have the chance to align themselves.

Be warned: by no means is this easy. This is most likely the most difficult thing you'll encounter in your life. You are slowly setting yourself free from old programs, re-connecting with the essence of who you truly are and how you treat yourself from one moment to the next. At this stage, you are non longer conditionally allowing yourself to love yourself, you are unconditionally doing that, and it's a beautiful and rare thing to witness in today's world.

LESSON 24—

THE POWER OF ALPHA

Your brain produces 5 types of brain waves: Alpha, Beta, Delta, Gamma, and Theta. These are electrical impulses between neurons that communicate actions, emotions, and ideas.

For the purpose of this book, we will focus this lesson on the Beta and Alpha brainwave states.

A person who spends most of their day feeling agitated, experiences sudden mood shifts, is often anxious, highly analytical, and who often walks with a sense of distrust towards the world and other people is in a Beta brainwave state.

A person who feels like their life has a sense of flow to it, does not experience low moods as frequently, has a boost in creativity, an increase in pain tolerance, and has great resilience to stress is experiencing life through an alpha brainwave state.

In our modern world of information overload and 'doer-ship', it's easy to see how we can over-value a Beta brainwave state while under value Beta. This is perpetuated by not placing our self-care and inner work as our primary priority.

We must begin turning our focus inwards and recognize that the mind, body, and spirit need a new direction from the decision maker.

The decision maker needs to assist the brainwave state on its journey back to alignment. Practicing humming through a 3-second inhale and 7-second hum, which also stimulates our vagus nerves to signal the rest and digest response, is one of a few powerful ways to move back into an Alpha brainwave state. Certain music and daydreaming can also help with this.

For our realignment to be effective, we must first begin to identify ourselves in one or the other main brainwave states discussed in this lesson. Above all, we must not immediately jump to what needs to be done, as this is yet another clever characteristic of the unconscious mind. Rather, as we begin noticing the need to bring ourselves back into an Alpha state more often throughout the day, our actions will become more often intuitive. We begin to allow ourselves to be guided by our intuitive selves. We allow ourselves to visit the creative alpha state more often, and encourage activities such as sitting on a bench as the observer of external things over and engaging in the noise from social media, YouTube, and search engines.

LESSON 25—

MOVE TOWARDS YOUR FEARS GENTLY

We have many fears we know about and many fears we don't know about. We tap into both through our feelings, dreams, and other ways. Today's lesson is about how to approach these fears, as the way we approach fear is often more important than how we react to fear.

Bully your fears into accepting a new perception, a new meaning, and you will only push experience back.

You must work with your fears rather than against them if you are to see change. A collaboration must be formed between new perceptions, new beliefs, and between a new identity and the old. This gentle and empathetic approach towards fears allows the unconscious mind to feel listened to, something that many people today have never done growing up. Your new identity must be someone your unconscious mind feels safe with.

Be the person that the younger you needed while growing up and over time the message of safety will get across the bridge of vulnerability. Through gentleness, through a new willing relationship that's being built internally, the unconscious mind will begin to accept that the fears it's been hanging onto are no longer valid.

LESSON 26—

TRIGGERS ARE VALUABLE PIECES OF INFORMATION

Turn the word 'trigger' into 'challenge' and you will begin understanding the roots of your anxiety more clearly. A trigger is something that we look to escape from, something we stuff deep down within us and hide from. A trigger is usually most overwhelming when it shows up as a physical symptom in the body, though it can also arrive as an intrusive idea or feeling. However, this is not always the case. A fear can arise from any of the unconscious mind's past memories.

As we move from interpreting 'triggers' as being dangerous to interpreting them as 'challenges', we sense that there is something going on beyond just the physical reaction.

We can now see how deeply our unconscious minds are still interpreting a specific time of day, an environment, an interaction, an event—anything—as a trigger. Change your mindset and the information coming through the body will now come in the form of a challenge that we can work with and that we can re-direct in some intuitive, positive way.

Through this new meaning, we will find that we become more aware of our overall vocabulary in terms of fear. This is a very important stepping stone in paying closer attention to the thoughts and words that prolong our anxiety. By replacing them we show our unconscious selves that these fears can be less threatening, and in turn, the unconscious mind becomes more cooperative.

LESSON 27—

PUT AN END TO THE MENTAL TUG-OF-WAR

When you embrace the decision to address your fears and anxieties, the need to grapple with a repeated, unpleasant, or threatening idea that crosses your mind at any time disappears. There is no need to negotiate with it, to beg it to stop or to distract from it. There is, however, a need to guide the fears and anxieties in a way where we progressively feel like we are getting the message across to our unconscious minds.

The less fighting we do with the fear-centered ideas that cross our minds, the greater the chance of relaying a new message—a new meaning—to our unconscious minds.

For the majority of people, this shift is gradual. It can take years to impregnate the belief system led by love and fear. As such, it takes time to guide this same conditioned part of you toward a new belief system. And it all starts with a less forceful approach.

Let go of the rope. Let the mental tug-of-war end. Surrender, because when you allow the mental war to end, you allow your selves to start on fresh ground. You

give yourself a new opportunity to make your unconscious mind an ally for life.

LESSON 28—

WHEN STRESS BEGINS TO FEEL LIKE A BEST FRIEND

During my retreats I often get the audience to close their eyes and sink into a state of complete relaxation. Once they reach the point of deep relaxation, they target where the root cause of anxiety lives in their body. This is followed by building an understanding of the characteristics of the fear and the anxiety's deep connection to the unconscious mind. These fears may present themselves in many ways, such as its color, the direction it's moving, the sound it makes, etc.

After the audience has had the opportunity to explore and get to know the root cause of the fear that has been compounding in this particular part of the body, I ask the golden question:

"Does this feeling feel like a best friend to you?"

This is often an eye-opening moment. A moment of deep recognition, deep clarity, when the answer is 'yes.' This often comes with the recognition that, at some deeper level, it has been they themselves that have been afraid of letting the anxiety go, and that they have had some need or reason for this best friend to remain.

Irrational fear, stress, and anxiety; each can feel like a protector, a best friend, a part of you that is vital to your success, protection, or identity. However, this is far from the real truth.

As you continue to realign yourself with inner peace, many of your outer relationships will slowly be replaced with new ones. The same can—must—be said with the inner relationships between the unconscious mind, the decision maker, and intuition. One no longer has supremacy over the others. Rather, all three parts are working in unison, allowing for each to play a part in meaning and action at just the right time.

So, my question to you is, are you truly ready to separate from what may have felt like a best friend for so many years? The answer must be yes, as there is no other way past this faux support than to intentionally distance yourself from its power and influence over you.

LESSON 29—

THE INNER VICTIM IS SIMPLY A CALLING FOR LOVE

Victimhood can strike at any moment during anxiety disorders and during the process of healing. I believe that the roots of an anxiety disorder lie mainly within a form of learned helplessness, a feeling of being unappreciated, of not being listened to, and a lack of love. I believe that many of the heart-related issues in today's world are due to this particular reason.

However, it is not anyone from the outside that the unconscious mind looks to for love. It is the conscious mind that must nurture and provide love to the unconscious mind.

It is our conscious self that must care for and love our unconscious self, the inner child when it cries for it. The more we look to other people to fill this need, the greater the distress we will feel. This is a vital point not only on the anxiety healing journey, but also in terms of the overall harmony between the three selves that one is beginning to recognize, understand, and tap into.

Your unconscious mind is a victim, and it is crying for guidance, care, and love from your conscious mind, who is now mindful of the fact that your anxiety is not who you are but simply a manifestation of neglect from listening and responding to the cries from the unconscious mind.

LESSON 30—

COMMIT FULLY OR NOT AT ALL

Anxiety recovery is a call to come back to a life we've been detached from for far too long.

The intelligent and intuitive changes we are implementing are done so with the goal of eliminating symptoms, reducing mental noise, and creating an emotional shift from negative to positive. These changes all come with a key question:

"What is the greater purpose of all this change work?"

As these changes begin to contribute to a new way of moving through this lifetime, we take away the pressure of recovering from anxiety and open ourselves up to the possibility of becoming supernatural. Our positive manifestation work picks up speed and our psychic abilities strength from this level of being.

These are good things. Different, yes, but good nonetheless.

Live and breathe the changes that you implement into your life and any path that used to take you down a path of anxiety will no longer hold any power over you.

LESSON 31—

EVERYTHING IS INTERPRETATION

Your interpretation of an experience is not the experience itself. It is simply your own movie about the experience.

The interesting thing about this healing journey that you are on is that as you grow to recognize the journey, you'll start to deeply understand that the mind's interpretations are false and that the intuitive self doesn't have interpretations.

This may lead you to ask, rightfully, the question, "Without interpretation, how would I be able to separate good from bad, light from dark?" This is where the beauty of a life in a flow state lives; the beauty of no longer separating the two extremes.

Life is always happening and we must choose to flow with the happenings if we are to find true inner peace.

Your unconscious mind may have just jumped you while reading this lesson with the idea that 'this shift in approach to life will only make us more vulnerable to external dangers.' This is a fear-centered interpretation. There is, however, another interpretation that doesn't stem from the conscious mind that comes with a question mark to its validity around life today.

For years I blamed my father for emotionally and physically abusing me as a child. Naturally, anything my five senses picked up in the environment related to him created anxiety within me, and this anxiety was usually coupled with repressed rage. This went on for years until I realized that it wasn't what happened to me as a child that was creating the anxiety I was living with. Rather, it was the way that I was interpreting what happened to me that led to the anxiety.

So I began to hysterically laugh every time something reminded me of him.

I engaged my highest self, my intuition, to force new meaning on these past memories. I found that through laughter I was able to change the unconscious mind's fears and find deep healing.

It is how you interpret the roots of your anxieties that will allow you to heal. So I ask you, what are you still holding onto today that you can begin laughing at and letting go in both mind and body?

LESSON 32—

INVOLVE THE BODY FOR TRUE INNER HEALING

The body is not just a suit of meat you carry around daily. The physical body is like a memory stick that holds onto all the traumas and highly emotional experiences you've had from past to present, both good and bad. It is the largest part of your unconscious mind and is a reflection of how your unconscious self perceives the world. This leads me to this very important personal conclusion in regard to anxiety recovery:

If we continue to see our challenges from solely a mental health standpoint we will never involve the part of us that is carrying all the interpretations that we need to let go of.

In my personal experience of working with others and in my own research, I've found that it is very difficult to truly bring mental, emotional, physical, and spiritual healing to a person without involving the body in some way. Moreover, I've also found that it is easier to enact changes to the mind through the body than it is to make changes in the body through the mind. To rely solely on a rational mind to convince the deepest parts of us that we are loved and safe today is next to impossible for a hypersensitive person experiencing an emotional dysregulation within their own nervous system.

The body must be involved in most of our healing work.

This can involve:

- Physically holding a winner pose while imagining your inner goals achieved.
- Placing your hands on your chest while speaking deeply to your thoughts, feelings, and body.
- Light walks while imagining that the fear is dripping off your feet with every step.

These are just a few practical ways to get the body involved. As you can see, in each example we are speaking a physical language that the unconscious mind understands. This goes much deeper than just a new idea. Posture, imagination, hands-on heart reconnection; all of these will get your new message across one progress-filled day at a time.

LESSON 33—

FINDING AUTHENTICITY ONCE AGAIN

When your anxiety levels in mind and body reduce it means that you are breaking free from the chains of negative habits that were holding you back. This is the time when people begin to tap into their true nature once again. They no longer fear interactions with people they don't know and instead begin to welcome these experiences. There is no longer a fear of their child hurting themselves as they play in the playground but rather a love that the child is expressing themselves through play. There's also no longer a need to fight for a set goal, rather there is effortless effort being put forth which makes the entire process flow from start to finish.

Once you begin to see your authentic self shine through, feed into it more.

Let your authentic self lead you. Let it be projected in all that you think, say, do, and imagine while allowing your fear of change to accompany your authentic self. No longer should your authentic you take orders from your fears; the tables have turned now. Your authentic self will now guide your fears and rewrite their meanings.

You have the opportunity to enact this every single day of your life from this moment forward. It's up to you to recognize the opportunities presented to you.

Always remember that you are much, much more than your anxiety.

LESSON 34—

YOUR PREVIOUSLY UNKNOWN STRATEGIES FOR ANXIETY

Has anyone ever asked you how you create anxiety and what specific strategies you use to create a state of anxiousness? I bet not. Today, I want you to pay attention to the strategies you unknowingly—and sometimes knowingly—enact that create the familiar state of stress and anxiety you experience.

For example, which of your five senses first picks up something that activates your fight or fight response? What do you see, hear, feel, taste, or smell upon waking up in the morning that creates a state of fear in your mind and body? Is there a color, a traffic sound, a reminder of someone else's disease, a smell from the garden, or the taste of, say, bread that does this?

What do you do right after this activation occurs? Do you touch a part of your body to relieve some of the symptoms you feel? Do you look for help from a support person? Do you go to your phone? If you go to your phone which social media platform do you begin scrolling through? After you stop scrolling and decide to take a shower, how does that experience go? Do you rush through it? Do you question the quality of the water dripping off your body? Do you question the ingredients in the soap you are using?

You see, suffering from anxiety isn't something that happens to you. It's something that occurs within you through your systematic and repeated habits.

These habits may not be the root cause of anxiety. However, they are the patterns that bring a person back into a familiar state of anxiousness. When you scratch your ear, rub your back, cradle your head, each action you take after an anxiety activation will propel you further into your anxiety.

Write down your strategies for anxiety at different points of the day, morning, afternoon, and evening. Start by recognizing these self-destructive habits. This is enough for now. And when you are able, focus on replacing these habits with actions that completely go against these old patterns. Learn to laugh at your fears.

LESSON 35—

FOCUS ON RELEASE INSTEAD OF RELAXATION

Relaxing and slowing down life's pace goes against the unconscious mind's orders to do more, be more, and prove more. Therefore, often when someone going through anxiety attempts to relax they are quickly disappointed at their inability to be in the present, to let go, and to calm their system for a change.

The key to reversing this frustrating inability to calm down is to build a mindset of 'release' over 'relax'.

As you walk on the beach you notice that each footprint leaves fear behind. As you lay down you recognize how your anxiety symptoms begin to rise in greater strength in order to let go of the pent-up stress that has accumulated in your muscles throughout the day. While meditating we don't look to bliss out but simply to allow the mind and body to do its release work.

The mindset of 'release' leads us down a path of allowing and witnessing rather than hoping for calm.

The attitude of releasing leads to relaxation in mind and body. From this inner place we no longer unconsciously place a timeline on how quickly calm needs to enter in. We are no longer frustrated by the increase in strength around our bodily symptoms. Rather, we are finally revealing more deeply what has always been information and messages coming from the unconscious mind.

By releasing our minds and bodies, we take a step toward relaxing and understanding.

LESSON 36—

THE DELUSION OVER THE SELF

The anxiety identity that you have begun to believe in is based on a mental construct that has been largely out of your own control. This "I" that you refer to is a construction of beliefs, imagination, perceptions, and unconscious actions that are centered around fear and protection.

In truth, your true identity and all that comes with it lies in wait within you looking for permission to play a bigger role in your day-to-day life.

This lesson is important in the way that we must begin separating who we think we are from who we truly are.

When you look in the mirror, look beyond the conceptions you hold about who you are, what your levels of self-worth are, your capabilities, and so on. These programs are limiting you, but they will begin to lose their limiting power over you the moment you reveal to them that you are separate from them.

Let love lead in everything you do, and you will soon be led to your true nature.

Question who you have become. Question the ideas and feelings that have brought you full circle back to anxiety.

Find the answers to what emotionally led interpretation has kept you away from organizing a new path for your life.

Your anxiety is a mental construct that till this day has stayed outside of your grasp. It is time for you to question why.

LESSON 37—

A TRUE TEST OF CHARACTER

Nothing tests the character of a person like unwarranted persecution.

An unwarranted attack, whether in the form of written comments, verbal actions, or an action from someone or a group, can leave emotional scars on a hypersensitive anxiety sufferer. These attacks, stored in the unconscious mind, can be taken much more personally than they need to be. Life looks completely upside down from an anxiety sufferer's point of view, and unwarranted persecution only adds a foggy haze to the decision-making one must go through daily.

Unwarranted persecution is always an opportunistic way for the persecutor to release their own suppressed and repressed negative feelings.

Once we recognize that these persecutions stem from the other person's negative feelings, we can give back the fear, anger, and sadness that we originally felt in those initial moments of persecution. We can see that the boiling pot of negative feelings, judgments, and labels has attempted to release itself by attempting to bring us down in some way. Therefore we must respond mindfully. We must teach the unconscious mind that we are not at fault. We must recognize that the other person(s) has tried to use this opportunity to discharge their pent-up energy upon you.

Overcoming this persecution and putting the experience behind us says a lot about how far along our healing journey we have come.

What was once taken very seriously and personally is now a fleeting experience. There may even be a sense of sympathy for the persecutor—a detail that cannot be overlooked. This sympathy sparks a moment of great progress, for when we no longer internalize the words of another but rather deeply notice where the accusations are truly coming from, we recognize our own strengths.

LESSON 38—

BAD COMPANY IS BAD FOR YOU

The people you surround yourself with will influence how you treat yourself. For better or worse, you will adopt the traits of the people you spend the most time with, and so you need to approach your relationships with increased awareness around who and which environments are using up your vital energy sources. Individuals and groups of people that emanate emotions and words around apathy, fear, anger, distrust, drama, disconnection, or blame take energy away. On the opposite side of the spectrum, however, are those who communicate with love, trust, ease, simplicity, connection, progress, and laughter will give out energy.

You must be fully aware of what forces could be taking and giving energy around you at all times until you reach a point where it happens by default.

At a certain point, the guidance coming from the decision maker will turn into intuition. At this stage, you will simply feel out what may be taking and giving energy. However, keep in mind that there are plenty of people in the world who may need some guidance, some wisdom, and some love from you as well.

Just like how the people around you will influence you, you too will influence the people you surround. It is up to you to decide whether a moment calls for you to help in some way, or leave.

LESSON 39—

TO NEVER BE LONELY AGAIN

To never feel lonely ever again we must nurture ourselves back to harmony with the decision maker. We must teach the unconscious mind to be comfortable in its own company so that we reach a stage where spending time alone no longer leads to a feeling of loneliness but rather just another opportunity to listen to what our physical bodies are telling us.

We are often hindered by suppressed negative feelings and to-do lists, and we allow the ever-increasing speed of life to take over that which we cannot be mindful enough to see beyond our immediate perceptions and feelings.

You will never be lonely again once you become fully present with your five senses in every moment.

To move past loneliness, you must be fully present in the moment. And to be fully present in the moment is to embrace the information flowing in through your five senses. The intention is not to distract from the past feelings of loneliness but to teach the unconscious mind to develop new perceptions and understandings in the present.

Embrace your sensitivity toward your bodily sensations and mental activity as this will allow for you to understand what sort of release work needs your immediate attention. The unconscious mind will hang onto things for as long as it deems necessary. It is waiting for the decision maker to take the reins and tell it what to do with this past information.

At one point in our lives, we looked to distract ourselves from spending time alone because it made us feel lonely and un-entertained. Now, however, we can begin to find release in our alone time and see the blossoming of this inner relationship as part of a greater purpose for us during this lifetime.

LESSON 40—

THE MOST CHALLENGING PEOPLE ARE YOUR GREATEST BLESSINGS

Often when we look to distract or run from the people that challenge us emotionally, we find ourselves brought back full circle to the same type of interactions within a short space of time.

Why, you may ask? Because you haven't made peace with the part of you that felt so overwhelmed by what the challenging person activated within you.

These challenging interactions are your greatest blessings. Without them, you would never be able to recognize what still needs healing within.

These interactions with challenging people are exactly that; challenging. However, the interactions enter you into a mindset that leads you to fill a gap between stimuli and immediate reaction. Within that gap, we have the chance to see the opportunity that lies within that very moment. When we respond mindfully, slowly, and without the need to entertain our fear-centered or angry parts, we take a giant step in returning to our true and unconditionally loving selves.

This will be one of the most difficult things you'll ever have to do in your life.

Since we're always looking for the easy way out—walking away or mirroring the other person's anger right back to them—avoidance seems like a natural response to the situation. However, everything we do will either lead us backward to our old core belief systems or forward toward our creative ones. The only natural step, therefore, is to face the challenge.

Intuitively you may already know how to treat these types of people. And you may do so from time to time. Now, however, it is time to become that person daily so that what started as fear or anger has no opportunity to continue.

LESSON 41—

THERE IS CONTROLLED AND THERE IS UNCONTROLLED REST

When I mention the word rest I am referring to alone time away from any sort of outside action, noise, or distraction. Controlled rest puts forth the need to control our thinking, react immediately to each bodily sensation, label an arising emotion, and to look to stop our mental imagery. By comparison, uncontrolled rest takes the position of witnessing the ongoings of the mind and the body without judgment and gives permission to the unconscious mind to release whatever has been stored within.

Uncontrolled rest will allow the body to do its own healing while controlled rest adds muscle tension to an already tense mind and body.

As we rest we must give the body time to catch up to the changes we are making to our lifestyle and identity. The least amount of conscious effort will lead to the most benefit. What this translates into is that you must see your rest time as a time to surrender. Surrender to ideas that float in and out of your mind, surrender to bodily sensations that increase in strength, surrender to emotions that want to pull you back into a state of 'standing on guard to a threat.'

Surrender, and you will see, hear, and feel things more clearly very soon.

LESSON 42—

THE FEAR OF REJECTION, THE CRAVING FOR ACCEPTANCE

So much of what we do throughout the day is for the sake of feeling acceptance from others. This can also be viewed through the lens of the fear of rejection, of our actions not being accepted by others. We dress how others dress, we speak how others speak, and we spend our time online and offline where others spend their time. Acceptance is then justified by how others respond to our presence, our words, etc. As a result, we find ourselves tippy-toeing from one situation to the next in a state of fear and apprehension.

Imagine, for a moment, that you gave yourself everything that you've been craving from others up until now.

The last place we tend to look for answers—for acceptance—is within ourselves. We always seek it in another person's special technique, words, supplement, pill, or otherwise.

But this does not have to be the case. Through active intention to give back and guide our unconscious minds back to perceptions of calm and safety, we begin changing in all regards.

Acceptance by others is no longer necessary and any future rejection turns into a fleeting experience.

Take time to reflect on this today. Be brutally honest with how you got to where you are emotionally. Only when you know where you are on your journey can you begin to rely less on the world and begin taking control of what little you truly have control over.

LESSON 43—

THE PATH TO SELF-CORRECTION IS LONG AND ARDUOUS

Change takes time, and do not fool yourself otherwise. Change work will take time—it may even take years of compounding repressed negative feelings, past reprogramming, and redefining personal labels. You are dieting the emotional body now, and with every new diet comes the time for the body to adapt.

What is interesting is the tension aspect of anxiety. For so long, we have been under the spell of muscular tension. It is present during most if not all situations we encounter during the day (and often at night).

Raise your hand for a moment and tighten it into a fist. Hold this tension for 10 seconds and then let go. What do you feel? Tiredness of the hand? Ease?

Just like the journey you are currently on, tiredness comes prior to ease settling in. You must give yourself time and you must see your tiredness just like a tightly-fisted hand that has to be let go. This natural progression into feelings allows us to feel like we are experiencing setbacks when in fact we are not. The tiredness will always come first; the ease will follow, if you allow it.

This journey is long and arduous, and it's meant to be that way.

Allow it to be as it may. Allow your conscious mind to send the signal to your unconscious mind that it may heal and come to accept change at the speed and time it feels is best. Do not force change. Do not struggle. Simply appreciate that you are on a journey. Anxiety healing is not straightforward because the path—these lessons—cannot be learned anywhere else. They can only be learned and adopted through through gentle and continuous process.

LESSON 44—

EXPLORE YOUR HEART MORE OFTEN

Your heart is the center of empathic connection, perception, and communication. It represents the center for love and security and is to be explored to understand its very beliefs. The decision maker (conscious mind) and the heart must find congruence, or else they will both revert back to what came first and has been the most familiar recently, meaning fear and anxiety.

Your thoughts and words are meaningless if the heart doesn't believe it.

This is where many anxiety sufferers struggle to father positive momentum. We explore our thoughts, our bodily sensations, and our behaviors, however, we rarely take the time to explore where all of this is truly coming from, the heart.

This work can only be done alone with a deep intention to understand. To understand what fears are held in the heart that prevent a person from taking greater leaps towards their goals of inner peace. The hesitations, the belief systems, the 'mistakes' from the past, all can be truly revealed with an intention to connect and to listen deeply.

Explore your heart deeply, without fear. Explore with a willingness to give back and you will understand why you unconsciously do what you do today at a much deeper level.

LESSON 45—

THE AFTERLIFE WITHIN THIS LIFETIME

When people think of the 'afterlife', they often think of a life that will come after their time on Earth. However, there is another afterlife. An afterlife that occurs within your living lifetime and often outside of your conscious awareness. This afterlife, the one that happens within this lifetime, is the life that you create for yourself after letting go of your old anxieties.

This new afterlife is like a rebirth. It feels like coming home.

And you must embrace this new afterlife. The people who question it are the people who find themselves reverting back to their old life—the one of doubt, fear, and self-sabotage. However, the people who truly embrace the new afterlife are the ones who will look back and decide to pay closer attention to what led them to this new afterlife, who may choose to bring back the doubt, fear, and self-sabotage, and they are the ones who can choose to oppose it at each turn.

No longer do bodily sensations mean catastrophe to those living in this new afterlife. We simply hold the messages to the conscious mind within ourselves.

No longer do we carry our 'mistakes' with us deeply in mind and body, as we now truly understand who we are and we recognize the value we hold. We project our value into the world daily.

No longer do we run from conflict or look to appease everyone we come into contact with. We become empowered and free to share our own thoughts and our true feelings. We look to guide our unconscious minds at each turn instead.

What we do for ourselves during the afterlife positively affects everyone around us more deeply than anything we could have done before.

If you are here, keep going. More sacrifices will need to be made and more discomfort will need to be embraced so that you can truly tap into your true purpose on this planet. You will find that the answer to this is much simpler than you ever thought before.

LESSON 46—

OUR INTUITION ENTERS

Your intuition is the most advanced version of you and initially also comes with a high degree of discomfort. It is the part of you that knows rather than the part of you that thinks it knows. For many anxiety sufferers, their intuition flashes the term 'surrender' at them whenever it comes into conflict with the conscious's demand to do do do.

As our intuition looks to surrender, the mighty force of the unconscious mind/body enters in and reminds us that we don't know how to surrender, that we don't have time for it, and that it's pointless to do so.

Your unconscious mind has an unlimited number of defense mechanisms to prevent any subtle push in a new direction that your intuition may give.

It's important not to label your intuition in religious or even spiritual terms. You should see it instead as your true inner guide. As you can feel, it is all forgiving—of you and others—no matter what occurred in your past. It is gentle, it is protective, and its messages are consistent.

The more we listen to our intuition, the better we become at listening to and absorbing its messages.

The greater the change, the greater the unconscious mind resists.

We are now talking about the greatest change of all: identity. Your intuition is always there to guide you back to your true divine self. As you learn and transform, you will find that you are not as interested in any sort of competition anymore, or any sort of exciting event that's coming up on the weekends. Rather, you are much more present, much more content with all of life.

The unconscious mind is dedicated to your survival and to maintaining old meanings and beliefs. Your conscious, the decision maker, is the one that decides where willpower, focus, and energy can be directed at any given moment. The intuition is the part of us that is unconditionally loving of us and all of life. It is the closest connection we have to our source energy.

LESSON 47—

THERE ARE NO MISTAKES, ONLY LESSONS

Mistakes are an opportunity to reflect and learn. That is all that they are. Since the majority of what we think, say, and do is led by the unconscious mind, most of our actions are not coming from an evolved or present place. Rather, our actions are from a protective place. A place where we are only looking out for our own best interests and to fulfill the needs of our survival drives.

There is no 'we' in this place, only 'me'. There is no consideration or thought of the consequences of our actions in the future. There is only the preservation of our present animistic needs.

It is time you put down the emotional weight led by past 'mistakes'.

Isn't it time to let yourself know that you were doing the best you could? This is how forgiveness happens. To come to the conclusion that they—our parents, our friends, our selves—didn't know any better either and their decisions were a result of programming from their authority figures as well.

This is your opportunity to release the tension you hold over the past mistakes you believe you've made. This tension may seem justified. However, the tension is only a fearful response to potentially stepping outside your conformity zones. You must begin to see it for what it is: triggers spurred on by interpretations made due to past experiences. Nothing more, nothing less.

As you let go the world will start to look different, and different is a sign of change.

Once you've let go of these 'mistakes', you can begin to move into the future with curiosity and optimism. You move forward as you did as a child before all the beliefs and labels that were instilled into your unconscious mind.

LESSON 48–

RE-PARENTING OUR WOUNDED MINDS

When I use the term 'wounded' I refer not to the physical but to the emotional. We are not broken, rather we are bent, and the way to mend ourselves back into shape is to take every opportunity given to us to 're-parent' our inner minds back to safety.

Sometimes our childhood traumas are obvious, often times they are outside of conscious awareness. Sometimes a life of chronic stress begins later on, and sometimes being stressed begins to feel like a normal way to live life. In any case, there is an unconscious mind within you that is paying attention to which thoughts you give priority to, which perceptions over your past memories you carry with you, and which behaviors you truly believe are right for each situation.

Re-parenting begins with intention, and our intention must be to be one step ahead at every turn.

Therefore it is not our unconscious mind that decides what meaning we place on things and what actions to take.

Rather it is the conscious mind, the decision maker, that decides.

When the conscious physical body progressively begins catching up on your tensions, it replaces the tension with flexibility.

And with flexibility comes the ability to open up to the guidance from our highest self; our intuition. Our intuition allows us to simplify and remedy—to re-parent—every aspect of our lives as we go.

Where challenges once felt like they needed complex answers, they now require the simplest of approaches.

Re-parenting is not always straightforward. Sometimes re-parenting requires an idea or initial feeling to be left alone, and other times a genuine and firm updated response through an action is required. Trust your intuition to do what is best in each situation.

Our goal is to no longer allow even one negative idea to blossom in the gentle garden our our minds. This can only be achieved through a willingness to move forward together as one with a brand new student-teacher relationship between the unconscious and conscious minds.

LESSON 49—

ANXIETY IS NO LONGER THE TARGET OF OUR INNER WORK

For weeks, months, or even years, your goal has likely been to lessen your levels of anxiety and eventually to stop it completely. However, when we look back at the results we've attained so far, we now realize that we've unknowingly fed into anxiety since what we give attention to grows stronger.

If we focus only on anxiety recovery we will get more anxiety.

All your change work must be done in present time. That means you are not doing something in order to receive something else—which in this context means to stop the elements that come with anxiety. Instead, we let the results be whatever they may be and we put our efforts into our emotional reframing work, our mindfulness approach, our meditations, the changes in how fast or slow we go about our days, and our lifestyle habits.*

If we focus on anxiety recovery too often we will become rigid in how we go about our change work, since our

expectations will be tarnished and this will send us back full circle.

These negative, unconscious programs within you have been in place for years and it will take time to reveal themselves before you can heal.

Do without expecting anything in return, change without placing a timeline on how fast it must arise.

Do for the joy of doing, as most people who are called to this kind of healing work will deny it and go right back to things that only provide temporary symptom-related fixes.

You are different. You open your arms up wide and allow the ups and downs to be there. You begin finding enjoyment and playfulness in your inner healing work. This is where the magic happens. This is when the unconscious motivations for anxiety begin to dissipate.

*Look up 'reframing by the anxiety guy' on YouTube for a video playlist.

LESSON 50—

WHAT DOES VICTIMHOOD GIVE YOU?

Secondary gains are conscious and unconscious benefits of the negative behaviors we enact on a daily basis. This is one of the driving forces behind victimhood. Someone stuck in the cycles of victimhood may receive such wonderful support online and offline that a part of them starts to believe that they may never receive this kind of attention and support should things start to change. This leads to half-hearted attempts during any sort of change work as change is no longer fully, consciously desired.

Often it is easier to stay as a victim.

Love, connection, being listened to, familiarity; all of these are powerful reasons for our unconscious mind to remain in a mental and emotional state of victimhood. And they will continue to do so until we begin thinking more broadly. Broad thinking encourages change because it forces our unconscious mind to think beyond the small comforts and securities.

When we think greater than how we are currently feeling, we can see that as comfortable as these patterns have become, there is something much greater awaiting us in our future.

Human beings will create change once they've associated enough pain with staying where they are or pleasure with where they'd like to go instead. This requires us to admit to ourselves how victimhood is keeping us stuck internally and externally.

This is not an easy thing to do. Yet we must start somewhere, and the best place to start is by being more and more focused on where your victimhood is taking you in the long run and recognizing how different this future self is from the one that lives with inner peace and freedom.

LESSON 51—

IF IT DOESN'T GO YOUR WAY, IT GOES THE DIVINE WAY

When mentioning the 'divine' I am referring to something greater than you. Not in an ego sense but in the sense of a protector, an energy that listens and reflects back to us what we give out. The eventual perfect balance between all things.

Throughout the day, if something doesn't go your way, it goes the divine way.

Meaning, there is a reason for why it didn't go your way. There are doors to be opened up in your future that you aren't even aware of right now, and as much as you wanted this very thing to go your way, it wasn't meant to. You see, as you change so do your inner and outer worlds change. You will find that as you go deeper into your anxiety recovery and identity work, strange and sometimes 'bad' things start happening. For instance:

- You get fired at work because that environment is no longer aligned with the feelings and vibrations you are giving off.

- Your best friend no longer wants to speak with you because your communication has shifted from negative to neutral to positive now, and you two are no longer an aligned match.
- Your car breaks down because for you to continue your growth you must begin taking your bike around. You begin noticing things you never did before and your epiphanies get stronger as you bike rather than drive since driving kept you fixated on all there was to worry about before.

In the beginning, it will not be easy to see this perspective when something doesn't go our way. However, soon after our initial disappointment, we can begin to free ourselves from looking to control what happened and allow things to unfold as they may.

Let go, trust, and embrace the moment something doesn't go your way. It wasn't meant to go your way.

LESSON 52—

BEFORE DESIRES VS AFTER DESIRES

The constant desire to be free from the elements of anxiety is the very thing that strengthens it. This desire comes from past patterns of 'doer-ship' that may have once been successful in other areas of life. However, in terms of mental and emotional healing, this approach only backfires.

Intention and desire are a world apart. Through intention, we can plant a seed in the fertile ground of the unconscious mind. This intention is gentle. It asks for the unconscious mind to be open to change and to slowly embrace the unfamiliar that arises through anxiety recovery.

Desire, on the other hand, uses up valuable self-regulating units (energy reserves) in the mind and body.

If we find ourselves desiring too often, we will soon find ourselves mentally, emotionally, and physically depleted.

As we give anxiety less energy, we learn more about it. Yes, the intention to change is there. However, the need to have it go our way today is not.

Healing anxiety begins where desire ends.

LESSON 53—

GETTING IN BETWEEN STIMULI AND UNCONSCIOUS RESPONSE

First, there is some sort of imagined or physical stimuli in the environment. This is followed by the activation of the sympathetic nervous system (fight or flight) or parasympathetic nervous system (rest and digest).

If that stimulus is of a safe nature to the unconscious mind, we will feel emotionally neutral and even pleasant. By contrast, if the unconscious mind deems the stimulus a potential threat—using the information received through one of our 5 senses—our stress hormones begin taking over mind and body.

However, in between stimuli and unconscious response, there is an opportunity for the conscious mind, the decision maker, to have a say or not.

Every anxiety sufferer today must see the golden opportunity that lies within irrational fear so that it doesn't turn into anxiety. Once the decision maker recognizes that their current experience is heading down the path towards fight or flight, they can choose to flow through the experience, enact physiological change (slow down the speed of walking and breathe deeply), or allow it to simply pass rather than give it the focus and energy it desires.

Intuitively, we must decide out whether it would be more beneficial to guide our unconscious minds in a new direction or leave its interpretation alone without feeding into it fearfully.

Both are conscious responses until they become automated. However, once they become automated, there is no longer a conscious need to get in between stimulus and response since a new program has now been set.

This is the main reason for the conscious mind: to give answers to the unconscious mind. For years it did not provide any guidance, it only went along with the anxious interpretations of events. However, we are now captaining our own ships once again, and soon there will be harmony between the conscious and unconscious minds.

LESSON 54—

A LACK OF WORRY DOESN'T MEAN YOU DON'T CARE

It is time to begin redefining what worry is. Our past authority figures (with good intentions) would worry over every action we took as children, which ingrained a positive interpretation around worry in our unconscious mind. Worry looked like something that would keep us safe in moments of potential danger.

However, this same positive view of worry is what leads us to unhealthy thoughts and perceptions when we encounter unfamiliar experiences.

Therefore we need a new definition of what worry is.

I will not tell you what definition you must adopt around worry. That is up to you.

The most important thing is that you recognize that this new definition of worry doesn't have the same meaning as the one that has unknowingly been in place up until this very moment in your life.

Worry isn't what granted you success, nor is worry the element that kept you safe from danger. As we begin attaching more 'pain' to worry, we can begin to separate ourselves from being engulfed in this habit.

Anxiety is painful, mentally, emotionally, and physically, and worry is always the provoker of anxiety.

What definition will you give to worry starting today? How will you make this new definition more real? Through what action?

The time has come to reveal the truths behind our anxieties, and as we reveal, we begin to heal. Worry is not necessary, thinking is. And they come from two different places within you.

LESSON 55—

INDECISION IS THE FEAR OF GETTING IT WRONG

When someone is having a difficult time ordering from the menu at a restaurant, they're questioning their decisions out of fear of not being satisfied with their meal. Similarly, when someone is asked a question and they cannot come up with an answer, it is often because of a fear of confrontation with the other person. To agree with their interpretations is a much simpler path than one of indifference.

The solution is to turn away from the old formula of 'ready, aim, fire' (which translates into prepare for, think it over) and act, to the new formula of ready, fire, aim (which now translates into preparation for a response, act, adjust if needed).

You see, you're already smart enough, intuitive enough, capable enough. You just don't trust that you are these things, so you put others high up on the pedestal of life and place yourself way below them. This is where the problem lies because, in today's world, the ones who speak up at every turn don't truly understand. It is the ones who keep things to themselves who do.

This is because the pattern of suppressing ideas leads us to becoming an observer of things, and from this standpoint, we can see peoples' true characters and gain wisdom from it.

However, balance is key.

There are times when it is right to speak up, and there will be times to be silent (not suppressive, silent). Indecision is no longer an option because we are now tapping into our true value as human beings. You know the answer to things, you always have. It is up to you to share it with the world each time you get the opportunity, should you believe that it would be the right thing to do for the betterment of this world.

LESSON 56—

THE TRUE WINNER IS THE ONE SMILING AT THE END

The winner in the endeavor is the one with the biggest smile at the end. Therefore, it is not the result that counts but rather the fulfillment that one gets from the process. To be truly present is a rare thing these days since the world is so very loud and expectations are endless. However, when you take a moment to be grateful that you 'get to' rather than 'have to' do what it is that you are doing, you will feel a sense of deep appreciation for the particular endeavor.

Another person may have taken the trophy but in the end, within a few days, most people will forget who the winner was. Today's breaking news is tomorrow's fish and chips.

We as, transformative individuals who have been called to do this inner work, must project ourselves as the winner no matter what. If you make less than your co-workers, you also probably take on fewer responsibilities at work. This is winning, as it leaves you with more time for your self-care work, for example.

Life goes on, whether we are regretfully stuck on a past experience or not.

This is the key lesson here. Everything is fleeting and we get to choose how we experience each of life's valuable experiences one moment at a time. Will you continue to be stuck on results or will you allow what is there to be as it is meant to be, with a smile on your face no matter what?

This must not make you feel careless, or uninterested, but rather evolved. Evolved beyond the need to have something go a certain way for you to give yourself permission to smile at the end of it. No, those days are now behind us.

LESSON 57—

EXPRESS MORE OFTEN. VULNERABILITY IS YOUR FRIEND

Suppress your ideas and feelings less. Express them more. This is a major step that every anxiety sufferer needs to take since they often keep things held deep inside of them out of fear of hurting others.

This doesn't mean that you need to speak of your anxiety with everyone you meet, as this sort of dramatic shift would be spurred on from a 'doer-ship' perspective. It means that you must take the opportunity to express what has been eating you up inside for too long.

Often, the most freeing thing a person can do is tell someone else how they knowingly or unknowingly hurt them in the past.

This is one such moment where expression would benefit the healing journey. Another would be to share what you've been going through and the progress you've recently made. This way you don't go down the path of total self-victimization, which would only confirm the lies fear, and threats of the unconscious mind.

Expressing creative ideas is another great healing step. As you speak about your creative ideas, your unconscious mind will look to reel you back into your old fear-centered comfort zones. However, the more you speak with certainty, the faster the unconscious mind will get on board with the ideas and beliefs coming from the conscious mind, the decision maker, within.

Stay true to your path. Speak up with certainty behind your words. Allow the outcome to fall where it may.

LESSON 58—

SOFTEN UP TOWARD LIFE

In our modern world, a hardened approach is valued while a softer one is seen as weak. In reality, this manifestation is more a result of expectations and living out what it is you want as if you already have it and not based on how much dopamine you can inflict into your day. We now understand more deeply that our unconscious minds do not hate us and aren't trying to ruin our lives through mental chatter, emotional numbness, or bodily physical sensations.

Since all of these are coming from a place of unconditional love, we can now recognize that the unconscious mind simply doesn't know the difference between what is good and bad. It simply does what it has been taught from the start and what has been practiced most often.

We start by softening up to all the elements of anxiety we've been fighting with for so long.

This softening up to our internal world creates a safe space within our unconscious minds to reconnect and re-guide without our conscious mind's involvement. It tells our unconscious mind, "reveal what needs revealing and I will guide you in the direction we must go." This is why inner change work often begins with heightened symptoms. We mustn't see this as a sign of setbacks but rather the release of the deeply held tension and stress that has accumulated in the body for too long.

This softening up to our inner worlds in turn leads us to softening up to our outer worlds.

We begin to be less demanding over others, less competitive, and less perfect. This translates into fewer 'willpower points' being used up in needless ways as willpower becomes replaced with allowance. The 'reactor' to the world's challenges turns into the 'observer' as we begin noticing that our anxious ways really didn't have as much of an effect on the world as we may have thought they did.

As we soften up, we begin opening back up to true and unconditional love once again. This is a major step in the journey towards total balance between the unconscious and conscious minds, and over time a deeper sense of flow will enter into all that one does throughout the day.

LESSON 59—

YOUR TRUE LIFE PURPOSE IS REVEALED THROUGH ANXIETY

As we evolve out of negative states and into more positive ones the whole world begins feeling different. We begin to look back and realize that we were caught in a long, fear-centered trance that we never knew we were in. We believed that our life's purpose was connected to how much money we made, how fast we climbed the corporate ladder, how close we were to our authority figures, and how comfortable our lives would become.

Comfort is the enemy of true inner healing.

True healing, true transformation out of negative states and into positive ones, is messy, confusing, and requires us to embrace vulnerability at each turn. Vulnerability then becomes an opportunity rather than an outlet to escape something. As we begin to understand the truth behind this potentially long and arduous healing journey, we are brought to the true conclusion of our life's purpose: to evolve out of the ego-centered prison we were held captive in for too long.

That's it, that's all there is to it. It is a very personal journey, and as we progress deeper into this work this understanding will grow. As we climb the ladder from one negative emotional state to the next, on our way towards that beautiful spot known as neutrality and indifference, we continue our momentum towards the positives.

Everything external is a mirror of the inner harmony of your unconscious and conscious minds.

Anxiety is a means to an end, an opportunity to see beyond the material and physical world. It's an opportunity to go deep within yourself and reveal what you've turned a cold shoulder to for quite some time.

As this recognition grows, anxiety will no longer be a 'bad' thing but rather a signal beacon pointing to where you need to do inner work. This, my friends, is a major step in your evolution, in you fulfilling your true inner purpose in this lifetime.

LESSON 60—

ALWAYS SHARE FROM YOUR TRUE FEELINGS

In a fear-centered world where so many of us are craving connection but only finding more distance between each other, share your ideas from your true feelings. Share from a place that is beyond the surface level. Share how you really feel.

If comfort is the true enemy of inner healing, intentional discomfort is the path to freedom.

We must share our suppressed ideas with those who have in some way brought us stress from the past, even if it comes completely unexpected to the other person. The only place a negative feeling can hurt you is when it's stuck inside you, therefore isn't it time to put yourself first?

However, we must be aware of whether our sharing is leading us down a self-victimization path as this is not beneficial in the long term.

It isn't a question of whether sharing your true feelings is good or bad. It is that suppression has been so familiar for so long that any opposite action will make us feel vulnerable at the start.

Maybe you feel that sharing your true thoughts and ideas is outside of your true character. However, I would like to ask you, how do you even know what your true character is when you've been stuck in a fear-led trance until now? The truth is that our anxiety has taken us so far from who we really are that the way back 'home' will take a daily commitment as this is an intuitive process more than anything.

Share your true thoughts about things.

Share your true feelings about the state of the world.

Share from your heart, not from your head.

Keep sharing until your authenticity begins shining through.

LESSON 61—

SEPARATION IS LEARNED, CONNECTION IS GENUINE

Watch kids at play and you'll notice how everyone gets along with ease. It is like a beautiful symphony playing effortlessly and in harmony with one another. However, once competition sets in, we unconsciously begin seeing our competitors as our enemies. People to become better then in some way.

Unless we maintain a certain degree of awareness, we will find ourselves distancing from others and feeding into our self-centered needs that we have been told are the most valuable things we can possess in this lifetime.

Competition can be healthy. It can feed the spirit—but only if it is approached in an open-minded way.

This would require empathy for the competitors so that we can recognize the healthy benefits of the competition rather than be led down the negative trace of 'must win'. By staying empathetic, we can stay genuinely connected to our fellow competitors. In this way, our path to unconditional love stays open. It won't be blocked by temporary desires for achievement, but rather remain open long-term to an approach where true effort in any endeavor becomes enough.

It is the tension and pressure of modern living that feeds into our sicknesses.

As politicians look to divide, we must stay united.

As competitors look to separate, we must stay respectful.

As life looks to speed us up, we must slow down.

As doubt starts to creep in, we must guide it back to possibility.

As separation looks to take over, connection must settle back in.

Connect and connect lovingly. This will go a long way towards living an anxiety-free life.

LESSON 62–

TRUTH IS QUIET WHILE THE LIES ARE LOUD

When referring to truth I am talking about directions that come from your intuition—your heart sense, your highest self. These directions are quiet and subtle. However, the greater our desire is to be led by this voice, the more impact it will have on challenging situations in the future.

The 'lies', on the other hand, come from the parts of the unconscious mind and body that scream the loudest, like an infant looking for attention. The infant continues to get louder and louder if no attention is given. Thankfully, even these screams tend to lessen over time as they continue to be denied the attention they demand.

The optimal opportunity to 're-direct' these lies is when their effect over us is neutralized. Therefore, it is necessary that no immediate action be taken in response to the overwhelming mental chatter or the heightened physical sensations during the day.

Always re-connect and re-build with the intention to form a new understanding relationship between the unconscious and conscious minds, and remain open up to the intuitive guidance from your intuitive heart sense.

Now is the time to separate between the lies and the truths, and stop feeding our energy into the lies with our focus.

The world is very loud and we must find quiet as often as possible.

That doesn't mean you must live in a cave and live as dedicated hermits do. It means you must reconnect with the voice within you that has been drowned out by the screams of your unconscious mind. Remember, the lies centered around fear are not necessarily 'bad' either. Some may be used for positive learning.

There is a very important unconscious motivation that drives each of these negative ideas through mind and body.

When the reason or motivation centered around protection dissipates and gets replaced, the unconscious mind no longer has a need to scream as loudly as it once did. This is where we hear such stories about spontaneous remissions in peoples' lives. Stories of people who have healed themselves of physical challenges through inner work.

See the lies, feed the truth, and be patient.

LESSON 63—

POINTING FINGERS AND BLAMING STRENGTHENS FEAR AND ANXIETY

Everyone is doing the best they can with the information within them. This is a golden rule to take with you throughout the day for the sake of ease and forgiveness. Blame can become a habitual act of the unconscious mind out of a fear of looking more deeply into the experience along with the fear of pointing the finger inwards.

We must forgive our 'enemies' before we can truly forgive ourselves.

Every finger we point at others is really two fingers pointed within since with anxiety there is constantly an underlying need to find something wrong with the world. We consciously search for it due to our repressed rage over our present circumstance, and we unconsciously seek it out of a need to fulfill the ongoing self-punishment programs running always in our unconscious minds.

Anxiety can make the world look upside down.

We tend to regularly misinterpret things under the influence of such strong stress hormones. What is safe

looks threatening, what is quiet seems loud, what is far looks close, and what is sweet tastes sour.

LESSON 64—

ANY METHOD CAN WORK FOR THE ONE THAT BELIEVES IT WILL

When a person believes at a mental and emotional level that level of belief starts the manifestation process. Therefore it is not important which method or approach you take to your evolution of negative vibrational states into positive ones; what is most important is that you believe it will work both mentally and emotionally.

Mentally we must *know* it will work. Emotionally we must *feel* like it is already working.

Notice I did not use the words 'you must *think* it will work' but instead, I used the words 'we must *know* it will work.' Thinking is uncertain while knowing is certain, and certainty is what will convince the unconscious mind to take on the beliefs of the conscious mind. This is exactly where many anxiety sufferers find themselves blocked; they are held up in their intention to move into the next stage of their healing.

Often anxiety sufferers 'think' something will work and therefore 'try' it. However, to 'try' translates into 'fail' soon after attempting.

For the one that *knows* it will work and *feels* that it is already working, this brings with it different perceptual filters. Here, in this place of certainty, the person filters out what could go wrong and is instead drawn toward what will go right. With these filters in place, the unconscious mind can begin deleting information related to doubt, distort negative and turn it into neutral, and end the generalizations that used to lead to so much anxiety from the past.

As you read this book, do you know it will work and does it feel like it is already working for you? If so, I commend you. You are well on your way.

LESSON 65—

HOW YOU IDENTIFY WILL CONTROL YOU

The unconscious mind will arrange your life according to your 'I am' statements. This makes them the most important words you will speak on any given day. An 'I am' statement sends a clear command to the unconscious mind, and we often assign great value to these statements in our lives.

Often we don't feel capable or deserving of healing. This is a reflection of who you have identified with being for too long.

It is not that something is either true or false about you. It simply depends on which parts of you you've unknowingly chosen to activate while simultaneously suppressing other parts.

With every 'I am struggling' message you send your unconscious mind comes the interpretation 'we are hopeless no matter what we try.'

With every 'I am embracing this healing journey' message comes the interpretation 'we are open to future change.'

In our attempts to connect with other people through our limiting words, we have grown to believe that what our lives are like today is the way it will be forever. We unconsciously keep ourselves stuck and anxious by not recognizing that we are limitless beings capable of finding inner peace as automatically we once found anxiety.

Identify with someone you can be proud of. Make your future self proud of who you are right now and always.

LESSON 66—

IMPATIENCE IS FEAR

When there is underlying impatience, there is the activation of the fight or flight system. There is a feeling of potential loss; a loss of control or the potential for something to not go our way.

We must ask ourselves, what control? Who's way? Who is the one within me that demands so much so quickly? What keeps this unconscious mind so inflexible in this current circumstance?

Instead, ask yourself a better question and you will get a better answer.

The more often we see things from the perspective of the unconscious mind, the more we will understand that impatience is simply just another defense mechanism of the unconscious mind.

To slow down on the road while driving and let someone in front of us gives us the sense that we won't get to our destination in time and that someone else is placed as a priority before us.

To cook slowly when guests are coming over may lead to them thinking we are unprepared and therefore make it seem like we don't care about them and the occasion.

To have to wait in line for longer than we would like may take time away from the next thing we have to get done on our to-do lists.

In truth, we have the opportunity to convert negatives into positives in the exact moment by noticing what mindful opportunities we have at hand.

When impatience strikes we must take a step back and recognize which part of us is impatient and make a conscious decision whether we want to continue to be led by this part or not based on where it's taking us. We have more choices than we think during a moment of impatience. We just have to mindfully choose.

LESSON 67 -

IF THE IDENTITY DOESN'T MATCH WHAT YOU WANT, YOU WON'T GET IT

Ask yourself, have you already become the kind of person who can fully accept your new and improved reality with certainty and gratitude? If the answer is yes then you are in alignment with becoming anxiety free. If your answer is uncertain or even no, you will find yourself wishing for better days more often than not.

The unconscious mind doesn't allow for a void to be present. You must either identify with being an anxiety sufferer or someone who has inner peace and freedom.

You may ask, how can this be done while mental and bodily symptoms are present? Firstly, the answer must come with a certain degree of realization that it is the identity that spurs on consistency and strength in symptoms since we expect to experience a certain degree of suffering from one moment to the next unknowingly. Secondly, when you have truly 'arrived', your focus will no longer be on the hypersensitivity of the body or the catastrophic ideas that float into your mind. Rather, you have now given yourself permission to be more present and more engaged with the world, and therefore, unknowingly, you will have created a new perception of your symptoms.

Many anxiety sufferers wait for a day that never seems to come.

If you find yourself waiting instead of acting, the stars will not align for you. You must first move through your day with the belief and certainty of what you *are* and by default what you want to become. At every given moment you are in communication with your unconscious mind. Therefore, you must send the kinds of signals that it understands. You must signal that the world is a safe place to live in and that threats no longer exist behind every corner.

LESSON 68—

SUFFERING IS A CHOICE

Things do not simply happen to us. What we project, we call back into our lives. Anxiety is no different. Often it is the unconscious mind that likes to point the finger at our boss, our family, our car, our living environment, our online presence or lack thereof, etc., to make it seem like these are the things that perpetuate the state of anxiety within.

In truth, we have unknowingly chosen to suffer in some way because our external experiences are changing to match what we have come to expect.

This is why it's essential for you to understand that anxiety is a process that happens from the inside out and not the other way around. With childhood trauma, for example, it wasn't the experience or the people in the experience that spurred on the core belief systems that keep anxiety alive today. Rather, it was the way our systems encoded the experiences into our unconscious that have led to anxiety. Again, inside out, not outside in.

Choose a different feeling. But this time guide what it is you have chosen.

Once you have chosen ease and flow for your life, all your external experiences will feel different even though they haven't actually changed from before. And if we continue to not receive the kinds of results we want, we must stop allowing the unconscious sides of us to lead and take power back through the conscious decision maker within. Choose wisely, choose with your heart, choose now.

LESSON 69—

THE ONLY MASTERY THAT MATTERS IS THE ONE OVER YOURSELF

The only mastery that matters is self-mastery. Everything else will fall into place as time goes on. However, you must know your outcome in order to master yourself once and for all. Often we are too general with our thoughts for this process to be understood by the unconscious mind. Specifically, how do you want your senses to pick up the world around you? What would you like to see, hear, feel, taste, and smell?

Self-mastery cannot start until we know exactly how we want to move through the world in sensory language.

Here are a few signs of self-mastery that you must be aware of. WARRIOR:

W - Lessened willpower: You are more accepting of things not going your way and therefore you let go of your tight grip over life. Less willpower is used, resulting in more energy going towards building the damaging relationship between the unconscious mind, conscious mind, and intuition.

A - Alternative perceptions: You naturally start to feel into new ways of perceiving what you once were dreading and afraid of, or angry or sad over, or disgusted by. The effort to accomplish this is lessened as it grows more natural so long as our blood sugar levels are normalized and we get enough quality sleep.

R - Reframing past: All your past traumas are beginning to feel like experiences and no longer like traumas. Empathetically, you see how your past had to happen the way it did in order to teach you what you needed to learn on your path toward fulfilling your true purpose.

R - Responses are lighter: No longer do you feel pressure to respond to someone in a certain way to not disappoint them. Rather, now your response is targeted at teaching your own unconscious mind a new meaning over something. Your conscious words become unconscious commands.

I - Imagining differently: Either as a regular daily habit or from time to time, you are consciously imagining a safer past as well as a pleasant future. This is becoming more enjoyable and rewarding as time goes on.

O - Open to uncertainty: Uncertainty is now your friend. You no longer fear the unconscious mind's negative patterns and instead, you begin to look forward since you no longer feel the need to control future outcomes in the same way as before.

R - You now recap breakthroughs: Before, everything looked gloomy filled with mistakes and catastrophes around every corner. Now, you pay close attention to your progress and recap the ways you expressed yourself, breathed deeply, and gave back to yourself lovingly.

Self-mastery must be our only focus here.

Do not let yourself be distracted by other priorities as these are all secondary. In time, what you've always wanted will arrive and often you won't even know that it has. But first, you must have mastery over your conscious and unconscious minds.

LESSON 70—

SIMPLER THE BETTER

During life with anxiety, we tend to look to complex answers for our healing. We don't believe answers can be simple because the analytical mind, spurred on by the motivation of the unconscious mind to keep things as they anxiously are, makes it this way. This leads to a feeling of needing to 'do something' at every moment of the day even when the simplest answer to healing begins with doing less.

If the answer is simple, let it lead you.

This may come in the form of adding a two-minute meditation practice to start your day off. Normally, you may have been doing six, seven, eight things in the morning in the hopes that these acts contribute to lessening anxiety (when in truth it has only fed into it). Other times you may get the sense that you can leave an anxious thought alone rather than look for some kind of answer to it online.

Let simplicity lead. Let it subside when it wants and speed up when it wants.

Simplify your entire healing journey by focusing on the clarity you gain from these simple daily acts.

LESSON 71—

THE FEAR OF LOSING IS HOLDING YOU BACK

This is not only true of unconsciously led motivations for keeping a person in an anxiety-ridden state, but also of consciously led reasons. We often choose to avoid looking at them in order to avoid admitting them to ourselves in the open. However, they are very real, and they are there.

It is often not the complexity of healing but the fear of an uncertain future that keeps a person back.

In our never-ending series of attempts to find certainty and security, we only feel more uncertain and more insecure. We are afraid of losing the physical protection that comes with anxiety. We are afraid of divorcing the best friend that we have unintentionally connected to in the form of worry. We are afraid of losing an identity that we have grown used to.

We are afraid.

We are just as afraid of looking directly at the root causes of our fears as we are of looking at the potential releases from them. However, we must admit the truth behind this fear. What are you most afraid of losing in connection to your anxiety? We as human beings will fight much harder to keep something we already have than to gain something new.

It is no different with anxiety. The unconscious mind can project a positive interpretation of anxiety to our conscious minds if you will allow it, and we must come to believe in it.

This is the essence of healing. This is the key. It lies within your ability to reveal what you are most afraid of losing, and ultimately letting it go for something else requires something you cannot tap into yet. It is in embracing this uncertainty that we find what we've always wanted: certainly and security.

LESSON 72 -

START EACH DAY WITH THE END IN MIND

It is within the first few minutes of the day that your imagination is most powerful. It is a time to use for the benefit of reaching inner peace rather than unconsciously continuing to run the same movie in our minds.

Imagine what an anxiety-free you would look like, what it sounds like, and what it feels like.

Before letting it go. No reflection, no analyzing, like letting go of a dove as it flies where it feels is best to fly to, you release what has been done soon after. There is no need to overthink this process as it is very simple, you have simply been doing it unconsciously rather than consciously for far too long.

You will not be perfect at it, nor will you even be good at this at the start. But as you gently persist, you will become the master of your mornings, therefore your day, therefore your life.

Imagination is far more important than knowledge or willpower when dealing with your own mind or the mind of others.

These deep signals will be recognized by your unconscious mind and the seed of a new identity will be planted. Always start your morning with the end in mind. It will set you up for what's to come.

LESSON 73—

YOUR CHILDREN WILL SHOW YOU WHAT YOU SHOW THE WORLD

We do not bring a child into this world to teach them. We bring a child into the world so that they can teach us. Most of us have lost our way. We do not know what to believe or how to act. And those of us with anxiety can make these things even more difficult for ourselves.

Look at the patterns of your own child and you will see your reflection.

We are directing them each and every moment of each and every day, often unknowingly and sometimes knowingly. There is no reason to be glum over what you see but learn from it since we cannot heal anything until we reveal the truths behind our fear-centered patterns.

Too often, a child goes from crawling, to standing, to walking, to running, and back to walking, to standing, to crawling out of fear.

Therefore, the words 'be careful' must be replaced with the words 'be aware'. Awareness is much more beneficial to a child than tippy-toeing around a new experience. Take a day to reflect on this and if you do not have children prepare yourself to be taught rather than over-teach. This way you are not only healing years of generational traumas but also extending a hand to make the entire planet a more pleasant place to live in.

LESSON 74—

BUILD YOUR OWN LIFE PHILOSOPHY

As we turn from being the frantic reactor to the quiet witness, we begin guiding our own lives rather than continuing to be guided by the voices of others. There is no need to overthink your personal life philosophy because it is already engrained within you. It's just that it is covered up with all sorts of other information that distracts from the truth.

You get to choose your true meaning at any given moment.

Something may look 'bad' to others that to you may simply look like a life experience that just happened. For every meaning the conscious mind creates within, the less opportunity the unconscious mind has to place fear-centered meanings on them in the future. In a short amount of time, these new perceptions and meanings around life become automated. We feel them rather than think them, which leads to less energy exertion in retraining the mind and body.

As a person's default emotional state turns from fear to neutrality, their intuition can begin to play a more vital role in their life.

As the feeling becomes fleeting, coming and going, a person will become 'higher' or greater than the anxious feeling. This is where a person will realize that the act of asking for something from their intuitive mind is wasted energy since what they have been asking for has always been within them. They just couldn't tap into it until the conscious mind—the decision maker—paved the way for this to happen through conscious interaction with the meanings within life.

Everything you ever wanted has been within you this whole time. Inner peace, freedom to speak up, a playful identity, etc. It is up to you to recognize that it has been covered up this whole time through layers of unconscious fear, and all you are doing is peeling back those old layers and enacting what is in line with who you really are now.

LESSON 75—

THANK YOU, ANXIETY

The anxiety recovery journey is no different from climbing a steep mountain and looking down to see how far you've come. When we can understand that anxiety is a means to an end and not an attempt to ruin our lives, we can make peace with it. Anxiety is fear in its most irrational form and sitting on the opposite side of the spectrum inner peace is unconditional love (which starts with you). Our anxiety journeys are simply us coming back home, coming back to a lighter, more playful approach to life and all its challenges, and knowing now that we've taken things much too seriously than they ever needed to be.

This attempt to recover from anxiety by pushing through the same frantic and lost self that continues to want to keep us in this state is a lose-lose battle, no matter how determined you are.

However, when we can step back and recognize that our approach must come from a different place, things will slowly begin changing for the better.

As progress and setbacks occur, we become experts on such topics as anxiety disorders, inner child work, and spiritual development.

As our gratitude for our difficulties from the past increases, the need for control and certainty around our current challenges decreases.

These are the very moments we truly start to come back into our true divine selves.

This sense of gratitude for the journey we've been through overshadows all other accomplishments we've met in our lives since this is a very personal accomplishment.

You may or not be here yet, and there's no need to fret if not. What's important is that you're on the correct path, and reading this book shows that you are embracing this journey wholeheartedly.

LESSON 76—

THE POWER IS IN YOUR TONE OF VOICE

Let's do a quick experiment together. Think of a negative thought that has been taking up a little too much of your focus and energy recently. Listen to what that thought normally sounds like in your head. Now, say out loud the same thought but say it in a much higher pitch, one similar to that of Minnie Mouse's voice. Say it again. And one more time.

Reflect now on how real the thought feels after this experiment.

Do you notice anything different in your mind or body? Are you less concerned over the thought now? Is your body seemingly less stimulated by the thought?

The power to change your thoughts lies in your ability to be mindful enough to change the tone as soon as the thought arises. In that very moment, you can create a 'state break' where the anxiety loop stops and a new direction can be followed.

Make this your secret weapon against intrusive thinking. Master it until you feel these types of thoughts no longer hold you hostage. At that point, you can stop looking to change the tone and simply look back to how your old self once gave these negative thoughts so much priority. From this vantage point life gets better, and better.

LESSON 77—

CONSIDER THE NEGATIVITY BIAS

Too often we place labels on our identity and mental health without considering the all-important negativity bias within us all. Anything that is 'bad' is four times more powerful to your unconscious mind than anything that is 'good.' Your neurology is designed this way for protective purposes. And yet this is what keeps us in a perpetual fear-centered trance, at least for anxiety sufferers.

Around 70% of the amygdala's cells are organized around negative stimuli.

Simply put, your brain's processing center for emotions looks for bad news first. When it finds bad news, itself and its partners, the hippocampus (which creates memories for the context of that bad news) along with stress hormones, respond to that bad news and place it in storage, set up for immediate retrieval should anything similar to it arise.

Positive experiences, on the other hand, have to be held in awareness and be repeated consistently to go from short-term to long-term memory storage.

Therefore, negative experiences are much more easily stored compared to positive ones. One is like Velcro while the other is like Teflon. This brings us to an important point of awareness: we are not 'negative' people, we are not 'going crazy' or anything like that. We simply haven't considered the negativity bias within us and we have instead fed into it unknowingly for quite some time.

The next time you feel negative consider the negativity bias as these facts will help take the pressure off. Soon you may naturally begin sorting for neutrality or pleasantries during your life experiences and no longer fall for the negativity bias again.

LESSON 78—

YOU ARE NEVER NOT IN A TRANCE

Many people are afraid to go into a trance. Yet many people also do not know that they were always in some degree of a trance throughout each day already. The part of your mind that is always in a trance is connected to the emotional state you default to most often. All emotions therefore are trance states.

Our job is not to get you into a new kind of trance but to get you out of the one you are currently in.

If we look at someone suffering from anxiety, their default trance state is one of fear and uncertainty. In this case, there are a few things I like to do with people caught in a fear-centered trance to get them out of it, such as:

1) *Get into their world. Show them that you empathize with their problem. This will unknowingly help them reveal the deeper issues with their anxiety.*

2) *Implement a confusion technique. This is where we create a brief confusing moment with the anxiety sufferer by giving them something they don't expect. For example, tugging at their tie, asking them about the strange object on the ground,*

splashing a glass of water on them, or even telling them a dirty joke.

3) *Once they're confused and engaged in a 'state break', you have a few seconds to get them out of their old trance and bring them into possibility. Ask them to share the same fear-centered idea but to do so with the cartoon voices of Goofy, Mickey Mouse, or any other cartoon character. This will take us out of the fear trance and into playfulness.*

Our goal isn't to get rid of the fear, it's to lessen the fear.

This process is so quick and powerful that I have used it on myself with great results. First I would empathize with my own unconscious mind (inner child) by placing my hands on my heart, then I would take a cold shower (state break), and then I would focus on all the facts that supported my good health (rather than be afraid of what my symptoms may cause).

Remember, you are always in some kind of trance. The question is whether the trance is supporting your healing path or not. If it does keep you in a negative state, break away from it and introduce a new state.

LESSON 79—

CHOOSE YOUR MENTORS WISELY

The people you look up to as authority figures will create the mental environment you hold within you, and that in turn is what leads to hyper-suggestibility. What this means is that you will question their words and guidance much less than you would the people you don't consider an authority.

The lyrics that are sung by certain musical artists, for example, go straight to the belief systems within the unconscious mind if, and only if, one sees the artist as an authority of some sort.

This is even more important to children.

The words coming from an authority are commands, not just words they are saying, singing, or relaying. This is why in today's world it is absolutely vital to check in with ourselves, recognize who it is we look up to more than others, and understand how they have influenced our belief systems and behaviors (whether knowingly or unknowingly).

Choose your mentors wisely.

LESSON 80—

DEVELOP TRUST IN WHAT YOU CANNOT UNDERSTAND

Do not get frustrated when you cannot understand something that you have spent quite some time pondering. It is not meant to be understood, and the more we mentally try, the more fatigued and overwhelmed we will feel.

Instead, practice the art of letting these things be what they may be.

For example, you may be searching long and hard for a reason why an anxiety symptom such as dizziness continues to stick around even after you've been altering your life from stressful to calm. Do not fret. You simply aren't meant to know yet. Just keep doing what your body asks for and leave the results to themselves.

Trust that whether or not an answer will show up, it is ok.

You will be at peace with knowing and not knowing. This is that magical mental state where you begin to receive energy rather than spend energy, which will only contribute positively to your healing path.

Your unconscious mind may force you to feel like you need to know the answer to this or that, keeping you in a perpetual state of fear and causing you to value intellectualism over intuitiveness. It is not 'bad' to allow this surge, but do not feed into it. Rather, trust in not knowing and walk the path that is more quiet and less noisy. It will lead to deeper wisdom.

LESSON 81—

SERIOUSNESS IS THE DEATH OF MANIFESTATION

Playfulness is power whereas seriousness kills manifestation. Some people confuse dedication with seriousness. Dedication is an ongoing commitment around a strategy that has the potential to help us in some way. Seriousness, on the other hand, destroys our mental resourcefulness, increases physical tension, and emboldens the activation of the fight or flight response.

We want to be dedicated, not serious.

There will come a time when you look back on your journey and realize that it was your seriousness that ran you down. You'll see that your seriousness is what convinced you that you would never heal, or you were too tired to put in the inner work.

Instead, bring a sense of lightness and playfulness (which both live within you, by the way) to your anxiety healing, and the number of choices you have for what to do in moments of stress and anxiety will increase. More so, you will see that it was the physiological tension you unknowingly put on your body based on how seriously you took your healing that played one of the biggest roles in keeping you centered in your anxiety identity.

To recalibrate, you need to listen to your body and find out which parts are holding tension (likely the same parts your anxiety symptoms are focused on), and begin letting them go. Tension dissolves each time we become aware that we're taking an experience or our own healing journey too seriously.

Notice, let go. Notice, let go. Watch what arises as you build this new skill. You guessed it: playfulness.

This is how I turned a monster (anxiety) into a fly (attention seeker). This is the mindset that will progressively bring forward the lighter parts of you that have been covered up for far too long.

LESSON 82—

YOUR FEELINGS ARE EVERYTHING

Your feelings hold the keys to two kingdoms: the kingdom of love and the kingdom of fear. Your feelings represent the core beliefs that lie within your unconscious mind. They may feel automatic, but remember, they are not permanent.

Take for example an anxiety sufferer. They wake up in the morning and instantly go into protection mode, spurring on a host of stress hormones and involuntarily delegating their focus to everything that could go wrong.

Naturally, this person feels on edge, doubtful, and afraid. These fear-centered feelings spur on secondary feelings in the form of anger—anger around things that did or didn't happen to them in their past and anger around the circumstances they have to deal with in the present.

This is an unconscious formula that we enact daily and it is what brings the familiar feelings we walk around with freshly each day.

It is certainly not by accident that we repeatedly feel what we feel.

Love can also be our default feeling state, but it does require a commitment to sacrifice many inner and outer comfort zones that a person has grown accustomed to. Feelings show the universe what we want to bring more of into our lives. It is a literal signal sent out through the electromagnetic energies emanating from the heart and led on by the mind.

As natural as fear-centered feelings can be, so can love. The key is to give love a chance, even toward those things that drive you towards anxiety, such as your bodily sensations or the constant mental chatter. Simply recognizing that these elements are just doing a job they believe is necessary (protection) will allow us to feel and accept them more. There will be less desire to escape them. Therein lies one of the most important lessons in anxiety recovery.

LESSON 83—

WHAT YOU'RE NOT AWARE OF IS STILL AFFECTING YOU

It's important to remember that your senses are always picking up outside information and looking to make sense of this information. What you are aware of you can change, however, what you are unaware of can change you—and do so quickly.

We must check in regularly with ourselves and recognize the state of our willpower points (how much willpower we exert throughout the day on worthy and often unworthy activities). As we do so, we can begin to notice the things that are eating away at our energies that we aren't aware of, such as:

- *People. If they are within your 'energy field', you are unknowingly communicating with them. The person with the greater intensity emotional state will bring the other one to what they are feeling.*
- *Electromagnetic frequencies. There are some people who are more prone to these frequencies than others. This can cause dizziness, loss of short-term memory, a zombie-like sluggishness, and slow learning.*

- *Music. These days the songs that are being promoted mainly to the younger generations not only come with messages that aren't positively supportive, but the sound frequencies and subliminal messaging are also doing a number on our mental health. Choose your cafes wisely.*

As we become more consciously aware of what we see, hear, feel, taste, and smell from one moment to the next, we can begin spending more time in nurturing places and less time in places that may be self-destructive.

LESSON 84—

IF YOU FEEL TIRED, REST MORE OFTEN

In the case of adrenal fatigue, nervous system deregulation, and even chronic fatigue syndrome, your best friend is resting. You must stop looking for the most potent supplement (although some can certainly be beneficial alongside resting), you must stop searching for answers on Google, and you must stop being so hard on yourself.

If you're tired, rest. And revert from thinking that you don't have any time for rest. The reason you haven't had time is because you've put everyone else before you. Now it is time to change that.

As you rest, dismiss any thoughts that come to mind around how rest is lazy, or how you're just not getting anything done while resting. Rest is what your body is asking for, so make time for it. In fact, make rest your most important priority whenever you are in a state of consistent overwhelm and tiredness.

Ask yourself, have all your efforts to stop anxiety been increasing your levels of fatigue? If you answered yes or maybe, then rest will be your best friend. For guidance on reaching meaningful rest, you can watch my surrender sessions on my YouTube channel*. They will guide you into a deep state of surrender that over time will bring tremendous mental clarity and emotional balance.

*Look up ‘Surrender Session Meditation by the Anxiety Guy’ on YouTube.

LESSON 85—

SLOW DOWN THE MENTAL CHATTER FIRST

Do not make the mistake of focusing on getting rid of the fear-centered mental chatter that accompanies you daily. This approach only strengthens it since by focusing on the mental chatter we create an environment that consists of competition when a state of collaboration is needed to form new ideas.

You must look to slow down the mental chatter, never to be rid of it.

This perspective is enough for now.

A part of you may be screaming out 'But how? How do I slow the mental chatter down?" However, the part of you that is asking the question is also the same part of you that wants to keep things as they are—anxious and fear-centered.

We must understand that any increased desire to fix something 'right now' will not come from a rational perspective or a higher place. It will come from a lower place, a place that simply wants to keep the familiar alive in your future. It comes from your unconscious mind, and your unconscious mind needs to be guided, not rushed.

As we begin slowing down our mental chatter we begin to see it as less of an enemy we need to escape and more of a disturbance that we can guide. From here, we can begin allowing an idea to spontaneously arise and guide it, rather than look to fight it or distract from it.

Slowing down the anxiety-inducing mental chatter has less to do with a skill to counter it and more to do with an approach to work with it.

It is the mindset that spurs the skill set. This is where the magic of long-term healing lives.

LESSON 86—

YOUR LIFE IS A PRODUCT OF WHAT YOU'VE REHEARSED

Life doesn't happen to you, it happens through you.

Once we can understand that our internal and external worlds are a manifestation of what we have rehearsed most often we can begin to understand how everything aligns. Anxiety, for example, is a result of the ways in which we perceive ourselves in the world. Right now, your understanding and awareness of this alignment between perceptions and anxiety is only just beginning to enter into your consciousness, and this is good.

No matter where you are in your healing you are exactly where you need to be.

Although you may have already recognized the lesson within this stage of your healing process, you may not have a true belief in it. For example, you may realize that the anxiety symptom you've been paying way too much attention to is a result of prolonged tension, fear, and emotions. However, if you haven't committed 100% to these connections yet then you will still believe that your anxiety is present as some sort of an illness.

You are more like a tiny boat caught paddling in calm seas in one moment, and then in crashing waves the next.

It is the crashing waves that are bringing you the sense of safety since it was chaos and drama that have been at the forefront of so many aspects of your life up to this point. You must make peace with peace. And yet, this is a new concept for most. It is not comfortable, nor is it straightforward. However, it is possible and necessary in order to leave the life of chronic worry and enter into the stage of true positive alignment.

LESSON 87—

TO LEARN NOTHING, LOOK TO LEARN EVERYTHING AT ONCE

The unconscious mind wishes to learn everything there is to learn in any given moment while simultaneously knowing that this path will only bring about more confusion and less opportunity for change.

This happens when we look to 'do more' for our anxiety thinking. The 'more' is what we believe will bring us out of our current state. In truth, it is exactly this 'more' that is the driver of characteristics we know as being 'doer-ship', and it is doer-ship that drives forward further anxiety.

This is our epiphany of the day: we must understand that the simplest way forward is the most powerful way forward.

There is no need for complex techniques or explanations. There is only the need to put our hearts into what feels simple. The simplest way forward is to begin calming your nervous system and getting yourself out of fight or flight. This could lead to sitting on a bench and breathing deeply, reading a book without the pressure of needing to read for a certain amount of time, or walking peacefully by yourself barefoot on the grass.

If we continue to consume more information from others in the hopes of gaining the insights we feel we don't already own within us, we are no different than someone who runs east looking for a sunset.

Look to learn everything at once and you will feel like you've learned nothing at all, remember this moving forward.

LESSON 88—

THE MOST MENTALLY FLEXIBLE PERSON WINS

To be mentally flexible means to respect all potential ways of thinking about something. The more 'hard-headed' a person is, the more anxious they often are as they look to defend their ingrained, narrow-minded ideas.

Someone who is mentally flexible does not feel the need to defend any specific idea because, in truth, all ideas could be potentially true, or potentially false.

If one person says to another person 'The color red is a bad color', and the other person questions this narrow-minded idea, that is good. However, if someone immediately agrees with the person's perspective that the color red is bad then this narrow-minded way of thinking will affect the person negatively going forward, both knowingly and unknowingly.

The moment a person voices an idea out loud, they are programming themselves to not defend against the idea in their future.

As you choose to be more flexible in your thinking, you will find yourself no longer easily led in one way or another.

This may feel awkward at the beginning, and the unconscious part of you will want you to go back to generalizations so that it can differentiate between threat and safety perceptions. However, you no longer have to be a slave to narrow thinking. You can free yourself by choosing the middle way more often.

LESSON 89—

EMOTIONAL HYPERSENSITIVITY IS A SIGN OF BEING OVERWHELMED

Often we do not realize how overwhelmed we really are until our emotions and our bodies begin acting very differently. It is like a quiet car alarm setting off a host of stress hormones and leading us to believe that the worst is about to take place while everyone around us is going about their day unbothered by the same car alarm.

We mustn't place the label that there is something wrong with us. We are just overwhelmed and very fatigued.

As we continue to prioritize ourselves and to rest more often, we begin the process of inner re-balancing. Tension will begin to lift along with our hypersensitivity, and we begin to see, hear, and feel things as they truly are and no worse.

Overwhelm is not a badge that signifies productivity and hard workmanship. It is a sign that you have neglected the most important person in this world, you.

Do not feel guilty for placing yourself first. Feel proud that you have finally tapped into the importance of doing so. An overwhelmed person will naturally look for more ways to be overwhelmed, just like a peaceful person will look for more ways to feel peaceful. It is up to you to take a few steps back and take a good hard look at your life now, and to see where doer-ship must be replaced with allowing and acceptance. It is up to you to allow life to play out as it may while accepting the outcomes that may be out of your control.

LESSON 90—

PUT AN END TO LOOKING TO PUT AN END TO ANXIETY

'Doer-ship' can come in the form of looking to put an end to the anxiety we are dealing with. Through this seemingly endless pursuit, we find ourselves overwhelmed and exhausted many times, and yet our way of thinking about our healing is exactly what will one day create different the results we are looking for.

If we simply look to put an end to anxiety, our daily focus will always return to some element of anxiety that we need to deal with.

Move past competition and toward cooperation. Cooperation will always take us farther on this path. Anxiety must not be seen as a 'bad' thing, because if this is the case then we are fighting with a part of us that believes it is doing its job. Instead, these protective parts of us need re-direction. And the best form of re-direction depends on the individual.

If anxiety ends tomorrow, that is fine. If it continues for the next dozens of years, that is fine as well.

It is from this place of disinterest that we begin to empower ourselves once again. By no longer the slave of an element of anxiety, and by no longer battling with a label we truly are not. Rather, indifference allows for authenticity to shine through once again.

LESSON 91—

DECISION FATIGUE IS A REAL THING

Every small decision we make that we could have pre-planned will use up valuable willpower points. Willpower is a finite resource and we need it for our everyday tasks in our modern world. Unfortunately, these willpower points get drained too easily for anxiety sufferers. Luckily, we can do something about this as well.

Instead of choosing what to wear in the morning, organize your clothes the night before.

Choose exactly what times you will be checking your emails and replying to people.

Have your morning self-empowerment routine ready for you on your bathroom mirror.

Decide what time you will turn off all electronics every evening.

Write out all your to-do's the night before.

The need to constantly mentally decide is a form of worry.

And you don't need to make so many mental decisions each and every day. As your heart guides your actions more often, the mental pressure is taken off. This change can feel very strange to start, but over time, the physical benefits will be too great to go back to the way things used to be.

LESSON 92—

ANXIETY IS PERPETUATED BY 'BAD' INNER STORYTELLING

Much of anxiety comes down to the types of stories we knowingly and unknowingly tell ourselves. Tell yourself a better story and you'll get a better psychological and physiological response.

When we were young we enjoyed storytelling. However, the stories by our authority figures always had happy endings.

And this is where a valuable clue to living a life free from anxiety lies. Each story you tell yourself must have an ending that fits with the way you want your identity and life to unfold. Tell yourself that the work day ahead ends with hugs and success, that you will tuck yourself into bed with a deep connection with the emotional progress you made on the day, and that your relationships will have flourished positively, no matter how challenging things may be.

Tell yourself stories of triumph and progress and always feel the reality of those stories in every cell in your body. Soon, your life will align with these positive outlooks.

LESSON 93—

BE WILLING TO SACRIFICE WHAT IS HOLDING YOU BACK FROM INNER PEACE

Too many people today want change but few of them are willing to give up many of their 'comforts.' Caffeine, reality shows, dramatic social circles, the news, video games, junk food, etc. Inner peace requires an inner cleansing of sorts. Not only of mind, but of emotions, physical body, and spirit.

Often when we feel like we are 'different' from from the rest of society, we are finding the true essence of who we are. We are finding peace within ourselves.

This sort of separation is what scares most anxiety sufferers into the 'fitting in' cycle. Inner peace to you is different from what it might be to someone else. Perhaps it is to be at peace with a warm bath at night rather than an action-packed movie or to replace coffee with chamomile tea. To go slow rather than fast. To love rather than fear. These are just a few examples of the many paths one might find on their journey to find inner peace once again.

The quickest way to understand this is to be brutally honest with yourself and see what stimulates you, sensitizes you, and activates more passion in your life.

Once you find the symptoms around the root causes of your anxiety they must be dealt with, either by being instantly replaced or by progressively distanced from them. Bodily symptoms are often the unconscious mind's scream for attention, asking the conscious mind to make a choice that no longer overwhelms or overworks the body's autonomic system.

Give up what holds you back, and in turn, you will naturally be drawn to a better replacement.

LESSON 94—

DON'T TRY, DO

Trying is a recipe for failing. Therefore, if this sort of language arises in your mind, you must question it immediately. Often, when we use words such as 'I'll try that new method for my anxiety', we are simply saying a part of me is comfortable with fear, values worry highly, and has identified with anxiety, and that I am too hesitant to see real and lasting change in my life.

When you put your whole heart into change, either:

- **A new** idea will form that in turn begins strengthening new neural pathways in the brain
- A new behavior will emerge that begins to prove how fear was sort of like being under a spell
- A new mental image will take root that has a greater potential **of being the outcome of a situation.**

We will then slowly release ourselves from the grips of anxiety. Often, when I speak to people who have healed through one of my online anxiety recovery programs they say how they did it. They mention how they first needed to become someone new before they could experience a body that aligned with their new identity. They began to heal when they no longer identified with anxiety, no longer 'tried' things, but rather they knew that what they were about to do was for the sake of their anxiety healing and that it *was* going to work for them.

This certainty was crucial in their anxiety healing. You don't need to be confident in your change work; you have to be certain. Certain that it will work for you. Certain that it m may not be right away, but it will be soon enough.

LESSON 95—

ANXIETY HEALING IS AN INITIATION BACK TO YOUR INTUITIVE SELF

When we begin experiencing something we don't want to experience, we must see it as a necessary initiation toward getting what we truly want. Anxiety is no different. As you go through this process you will be very uncomfortable. However, you get to choose which type and what level of discomfort you are in from one day to the next.

You can either be uncomfortably fearful, or you can be uncomfortably vulnerable.

For example, say you get on a plane and you dread the feeling of not having control over the plane itself. You can approach this experience from a fear-centered discomfort where you hope everything goes alright and that you survive the trip, which would be highly uncomfortable, to say the least. Or you can approach the plane trip in a way where you recognize that in order to become who you say you want to become, you must first be ready to accompany your bodily symptoms and mental chatter within the new identity you already have within you.

You must give up control to gain control. You must see your anxiety as fragments of your past fears that are clinging onto you and that you no longer have to listen to its guidance.

Each new day brings with it another opportunity to go through this initiation process with grace and faith. Soon anxiety will no longer be something that you dread, but rather something that you allow to be there when you choose, and with as much attention as you decide.

LESSON 96—

INTEND TO RELEASE RATHER THAN HOPING TO RELAX

It is only natural for someone suffering from anxiety to wish for a more peaceful and relaxed present experience. When in the grips of anxiety, most of what we do throughout the day is based around trying to relax from potential threats and calm the body back into balance. However, often this becomes a self-destructive habit. A frustrating one that we must learn from and look to alter.

The next time any element of anxiety such as bodily sensations arises, you must see it as a form of physiological release. This will help you neutralize the feeling you are having.

The more often we allow our bodies to release, the greater our chance to find inner peace. Once again, this turns us away from 'doer-ship' and toward the silent witness of inner happenings.

This is a mindset. One of allowance over the need to control and micromanage each element of anxiety we experience. This idea of seeing the elements of anxiety as forms of releasing suppressed feelings and compounded stress allows the body to do what it does best: heal.

It is the analytical mind that gets in the way of this healing. Focus on releasing what arises as you accompany the mind and body through this period of unconscious expression. Soon, you will naturally begin to feel more relaxed.

LESSON 97—

PAIN IS NOT A MEANS TO A REWARDING END

Many of us have had the experience of going through deep levels of mental, emotional, and even physical pain during our childhood, to the point where our unconscious minds feel that the pain is needed for the reward to be achieved. It is this constant pushing that leads us to the pain we become so accustomed to and which we believe is necessary for us to receive some type of reward.

However, you no longer have to suffer in order to find mental clarity, emotional ease, and physical healing. Your ability to heal is already there, you simply have to tap into it rather than continue to fight it.

You see, with anxiety healing, it is not that we are *becoming* or *feeling* something that we never have before. We are simply *allowing* what has always been within us to shine through once again. The endless YouTube videos on anxiety content, endless reading of books on mental health, the endless sharing of mental and emotional pains on online forums; all of this can now stop as we have recognized that it was this very level of doer-ship that was keeping us from the truth all this time.

The truth is that pain is not a prerequisite for healing. This is a delusional idea brought on by the unconscious mind as it looks to use all its tricks to keep us protected from change.

LESSON 98—

DECIDE OR YOUR UNCONSCIOUS MIND WILL DECIDE FOR YOU

The unconscious mind bases its beliefs and actions on information gathered by the senses during past experiences. Its belief system is separate from that of the conscious mind, the decision maker. This belief system reigns supreme and decides all unconscious actions throughout each of our days until our awareness of these patterns increases.

If you do not decide what something really means, your past will decide for you.

If you do not act in a way that opposes the protective fear-centered belief systems of your unconscious mind, what you fear now will grow in strength over time.

If you do not see, hear, and feel things from a more loving perspective, the fog of anxiety will never lift.

You see, in the end, it is our decisions that shape meaning, and it is the meaning we give that shapes how we feel.

Your life is not pre-determined in any which way. Your life is a reflection of the choices you have mostly made unknowingly. Until today, that is. Because today you get to look at the underlying meanings that perpetuate your anxiety and decide on new meanings for them.

In a short time, you may find yourself becoming compassionate towards the elements of anxiety that have taken so much of your life experience away from you in the past. Compassion starts with you and it starts within. With compassion comes forgiveness. Forgiveness for yourself for going through a chapter with such deep levels of stress. You are forgiven.

LESSON 99—

SETBACKS ARE GOOD

An inner setback is the feeling we get when we feel like we don't deserve something. It is a feeling that has built up to the point where we experience more mental, emotional, or physical stress than we'd like. Setbacks, however, are sometimes more important than positive progress since we have the opportunity to reflect on these setbacks and see where we may have drifted too far away from our true path.

Setbacks are not bad. They are simply information to become aware of.

Maybe we got caught up in the latest news.

Maybe we spend too much time in front of a TV screen or mobile phone.

Maybe we took on too much today.

Setbacks often occur right after great inner progress has been made. The feeling of normalcy takes over and we tell ourselves, 'Now I can have that coffee I had to give up for far too long.' It is at that moment that the body replies with the idea that it is, in fact, *not* ready for such a dramatic change yet.

See your inner setbacks as an important aspect of your inner change work and you will never be disappointed with yourself again. You will be encouraged by what your setbacks uncover rather than continuing to feed yourself the needless idea that you're going right back to the beginning of this healing process.

Setbacks show us the progress we have made as well as the progress we have yet to make.

LESSON 100—

EVERYTHING WILL BEGIN TO FEEL DIFFERENT

As the transition from uncontrolled fear to unconditional love becomes more evident, life will begin to look very different. You will begin to feel like you no longer 'need' the people closest to you and instead, you will feel that they are a beautiful addition to your personal journey. You will begin questioning societal norms and systems more often, and in turn, this will allow you to disconnect from the way others go about their days. You will begin emphasizing positive alignment with your life goals rather than on all the little details that demand to be examined in painful detail.

Life will feel like it is on your side.

And when this happens, move with it. Stress and struggle may seem familiar, control may seem necessary, and the need to know the answer to something immediately may feel urgent. However, you now realize that everything you ever wanted can only arise through a balance of it all.

Certain aspects of your life will feel like they are coming apart. This is simply to make space for what is to come.

A positive person cannot have a negative environment and a negative person cannot have a positive environment. We draw in what we give out through the way we feel so our external world will always be a reflection of our internal world.

You are loved, you are appreciated, you are accepted. Welcome to the truth of things.

LESSON 101—

BE GENTLE IN ALL YOU DO

Do your best as a mother or father, and that is enough for your children. Do your best to guide your unconscious mind back to safety and away from perceived threat, and that is enough for you. Do your best to spread hope to the world, and that is enough for us all.

By the act and intention of inner healing, you heal the world.

Just as dominos fall one after another, you are already making a positive impact on this world, and for that I commend you. Thank you for making the choice to question your irrational fears and give light to optimism and consciousness. Thank you for the gentle thoughts, words, and actions that leave you fulfilled beyond your wildest dreams, since what you are going through right now is the true purpose for you and your life. Everything else is truly next to meaningless in the big picture of life.

Allow things to change as they do without forcefulness and you will have it. Stay aware, stay blessed, and stay with love, my peaceful warrior.

CONCLUSION

Your commitment to making it this far is commendable, so well done. From here on you may trust in your intuitive sense to guide you toward the next step on your personal journey towards inner peace. As you begin to move away from negative emotional states to positive states, you will find that the inner and outer challenges don't necessarily go away.

You just get better and better at re-perceiving them, seeing them for what they really are, and dealing with them.

The universe will test you every single day. These outer tests will lead to inner tests in the form of bodily sensations, negative feelings, and old thoughts creeping up. To go beyond these is to acknowledge these for what they are: outdated pieces of information coming from the unconscious mind as it looks to see if they should truly be let go or not.

Self-mastery is the only form of mastery that truly matters in this lifetime.

Perceiving the old anxiety 'monster' as a fly takes a willingness to recognize that the only reason we saw it as a monster in the first place was because we fed it our focus, our energy, and our identity.

What we feed into becomes our reality.

You will find that as time goes on you are no longer distracted from or running from what is now a fly, an unconscious thought form, but instead you respect the unconscious thought for what it has been trying to do for you.

The unconscious mind never knew whether what it was portraying as thought, feeling, sensation, mental imagery, or otherwise was a good or bad thing. It was doing what it believed was the right thing to do to protect and preserve an identity that we unknowingly believed we had.

As time goes on, you will find that you are no longer focused on preventing or healing your stress and anxiety. You are now more focused on living through the guidance of your intuitive, conscious self.

As the overflowing cup that used to contain all of the unconscious mind's beliefs begins to empty, we begin to make space for conscious guidance.

As we consistently become more aware of what is true and what is a repeated idea, we open up space for our intuition, our heart sense, to guide us.

Soon enough we will recognize that most of our past worries were just keeping us preoccupied and never truly came true.

From here on you have momentum. Like a train picking up speed, you are coming into your own.

To control each and every thought that crosses your mind is no longer necessary. To find answers to what each bodily sensation means is simply tiresome, and to believe that your unconsciously-led imagination is a sign of what will take place in your future is completely misleading.

Allow things to become clearer to you. As time goes on, you will leave the need for 'doer-ship' behind you for good.

You will find that what you truly want and what you truly deserve happens more naturally than you ever thought could. At this point, you are in alignment with love and gratitude. From here, you become a shining light for others to naturally join. You give others permission to become authentic once again.

You are becoming the peaceful warrior you always knew you were. I love you, thank you.

Dennis

Printed in Dunstable, United Kingdom

66906882R00129